The Bathroom Joke ALMANAC

Compiled by the Lavatorial Staff of Red-Letter Press:

"Head" Jokesters:
Russ "The Flush" Edwards and Jack Kreismer

Significant Others: Angela Demers,
Ellen Fischbein and Geoff Scowcroft

Cover and Page Design:
Fred and Diane Swartz

RED-LETTER PRESS, INC.

Saddle River, New Jersey

THE BATHROOM JOKE ALMANAC

ISBN: 0-940462-63-X

Printed in the United States of America

For information address Red-Letter Press, Inc.
P.O. Box 393, Saddle River, N.J. 07458

January 1st

TODAY'S THOUGHT: "You can't have everything. Where would you put it?" —*Steven Wright*

OBSERVANCE/EVENT: January is "National Prune Breakfast Month", "National Oatmeal Month" and "National Fiber Focus Month" so since you're reading the Bathroom Joke Almanac, you're obviously right on top of things!

Graffiti
Time wounds all heels!

JOKE: The difference between an optimist and a pessimist is that an optimist stays up New Year's Eve to see the new year in and the pessimist stays up to make sure the old one left.

January 2nd

TODAY'S THOUGHT: "Gossip is where you hear something you like about someone you don't." —*Earl Wilson*

OBSERVANCE/EVENT: In 1959 Soviet Space Probe Luna 1 missed the moon and went into orbit around the sun. All those years we sweated their missiles and these guys couldn't even shoot the MOON!!

Graffiti
I used up all my sick days so I called in dead.

JOKE: Two army recruits are waiting in line to be vaccinated. One turns to his buddy and says, "What an outfit. We've only been in the Army for ten minutes and already we're presenting arms!"

January 3rd

TODAY'S THOUGHT: "Laughter is the shortest distance between two people." —*Victor Borge*

OBSERVANCE/EVENT: On this day in 1909, Victor Borge was born Borge Rosenbaum.

Graffiti
The Ten Commandments aren't multiple-choice.

JOKE: A man was spread out over three seats in the third row of a movie theater. The usher came by and said, "It's very inconsiderate of you to be taking up three seats. Where did you come from anyway?" The man looked up at the usher and groaned, "The balcony."

January 4th

TODAY'S THOUGHT: "Just when I found out the meaning of life, they changed it." —*George Carlin*

OBSERVANCE/EVENT: It's "Trivia Day", an annual observance to honor folks who know things like it's Independence Day in Burma, General Tom Thumb was born on this day in 1838, and the fact that today is "Trivia Day".

Graffiti
Square bathtubs don't have rings.

JOKE:

Q: What do you call a cow with only two legs?
A: *Lean beef*

January 5th

TODAY'S THOUGHT: "My father once tried to play *Flight of the Bumblebee* on the tuba. Blew his liver through the horn." —*Woody Allen*

OBSERVANCE/EVENT: It's "Twelfth Night", the end of Christmas and time to take all those geese a-laying, turtledoves and pipers piping that your true love gave to you back for an exchange.

Graffiti

The days of the digital watch are numbered!

JOKE: Speaking of pipers piping, a plumber built up quite a business in Las Vegas specializing in casino bathrooms. His slogan was "A Flush Is Better Than A Full House".

January 6th

TODAY'S THOUGHT: "A lot of people like snow. I find it unnecessary freezing of water." —*Carl Reiner*

OBSERVANCE/EVENT: Danny Thomas was born in 1914. Comedians all around the globe are giving a 21 spit-take salute in his memory.

Graffiti

Miracle Drug —
one that keeps you alive until you pay off the bill.

JOKE: Two caterpillars are talking to one another when, all of the sudden, a butterfly goes by. The first caterpillar says to the second, "You'll never get me up in one of those things."

January 7th

TODAY'S THOUGHT: "It was so cold that politicians were walking around with their hands in their own pockets." —*Bob Hope*

OBSERVANCE/EVENT: Millard Fillmore, the 13th president, was born on this day in 1800. His Know-Nothing Party didn't contribute much to history but Millard's birthday provides a great excuse to hold a party.

Graffiti
My Karma ran over your Dogma.

JOKE:

Q: Where was the crossword puzzle inventor buried?
A: *6' down, 3' across*

January 8th

TODAY'S THOUGHT: "Ever wonder if illiterate people get the full effect of alphabet soup?" —*John Mendoza*

OBSERVANCE/EVENT: Speaking of soup, Soupy Sales was born on this day in 1930 in Wake Forest, North Carolina because, as Soupy puts it, "I wanted to be near my mother."

Graffiti
Every town has gossip. If you don't hear it, you're it.

JOKE: Two commuters struck up a conversation.
"I have four children," said one man proudly.
"Oh my, I wish I had four children," sighed the other.
"Don't you have any children?" asked his new friend sympathetically.
"Yeah, eight."

January 9th

TODAY'S THOUGHT: "I'd like to come back as an oyster. Then I'd only have to be good September through April." —*Gracie Allen*

OBSERVANCE/EVENT: They're hoisting a few fermented coconut milks on Gilligan's Island today in celebration of Bob Denver's birthday. Bob was born in New Rochelle, New York in 1935.

> **Graffiti**
> *Seconds count...especially when dieting.*

JOKE:

Q: What do you get if you cross a lawyer with a snake?

A: *A disgusted snake*

January 10th

TODAY'S THOUGHT: "I never got respect. I remember when I was a kid and played hide and seek...they wouldn't even look for me." —*Rodney Dangerfield*

OBSERVANCE/EVENT: Celebrate "Where's The Beef? Day". Wendy's cooked up this famous spot in 1984 and it really put them on a roll.

> **Graffiti**
> *He who hesitates loses his parking space!*

JOKE: Two atoms are walking down the street and one says, "I've been thinking. There's no doubt that I'm an ion."

"Are you sure?" asked the other atom incredulously.

"Yes, I'm positive."

January 11th

TODAY'S THOUGHT: "Did you ever hear someone say this: It was more fun than a barrel of monkeys. Did you ever ***smell*** a barrel of monkeys?" —*Steve Bluestein*

OBSERVANCE/EVENT: In 1963 Whiskey-A-Go-Go, the first American discotheque, opened in L.A. The original crowd is planning a reunion in the near future. It will be held at the Prune Juice-A-Go-Go.

Graffiti

Aan aardvark is aan aanimal like aan aanteater.

JOKE:

Q: What's the difference between a fly and a mosquito?

A: *You can't zip a mosquito.*

January 12th

TODAY'S THOUGHT: "I just got back from a pleasure trip. I took my mother to the airport."
—*Henny Youngman*

OBSERVANCE/EVENT: Just a reminder that January is "National Careers In Cosmetology Month". There's still time to enroll in a beauty school although you might have to take a couple of make-up tests. (Now it's also officially "Stupid Pun Day".)

Graffiti

Stucco — what you get when you sit on gummo.

JOKE:

Q: What do you get from a pet dog and a pet chicken?

A: *Barkin' and eggs*

January 13th

TODAY'S THOUGHT: "Be fair with others but then keep after them until they're fair with you."
—*Alan Alda*

OBSERVANCE/EVENT: In 1910, Lee Deforest conducted the first radio broadcast to the public. Little did Deforest realize that all those cat's whiskers, crystals and primitive vacuum tubes would lead to the invention of Howard Stern.

Graffiti
A will is a dead giveaway.

JOKE: "Cheer up, Dad," said the wiseacre teen. "Don't think of it as going bald. You're just taller than your hair."

January 14th

TODAY'S THOUGHT: "According to statistics, a man eats a prune every twenty seconds. I don't know who this fellow is, but I know where to find him."
—*Morey Amsterdam*

OBSERVANCE/EVENT: Andy Rooney let out his first whine on this date back in 1919. "Didja ever wonder why obstetricians have to slap you so hard?"

Graffiti
They call it "revolving credit" because the interest makes your head spin!

JOKE:

Q: What are the last two words of the *Star Spangled Banner?*

A: *"Play Ball!"*

January 15th

TODAY'S THOUGHT: "If you're going to tell people the truth, be funny or they'll kill you." —*Billy Wilder*

OBSERVANCE/EVENT: Radio wit and top comedy writer Goodman Ace was born in 1899.

Graffiti
Saints teach their dogs to heal.

JOKE: "Doctor, you've got to help me!" said the excited young man to the psychiatrist. "I keep imagining my body is covered in gold."
"Don't worry about a thing," answered the shrink. "It's very common. You have what we call a gilt complex."

January 16th

TODAY'S THOUGHT: "An actor's a guy who, if you ain't talking about him, he ain't listening."
—*Marlon Brando*

OBSERVANCE/EVENT: It's "National Nothing Day" so if you've got nothing planned, you're right in keeping with the spirit of the occasion.

Graffiti
An ape is the only other animal that kisses.

JOKE:

Q: What did the teacher say when her glass eye fell out and went down the drain?

A: *"Oh, no, I've lost another pupil."*

January 17th

TODAY'S THOUGHT: "Buy thermometers in the wintertime. They're much lower then."—*Soupy Sales*

OBSERVANCE/EVENT: One our favorite funny females, Betty White, was born today in 1928.

Graffiti

The Domino Theory: Eat Enough Pizza And You'll Fall Over.

JOKE: A father had unexpectedly dropped in on his son at the college dorm.

"Son, I've been coming down here every weekend and keeping an eye on you. You're always going to wild parties, drinking and carousing with loose women. Don't you know what good clean fun is?"

"No, Dad," answered his smart-aleck son. "What good is it?"

January 18th

TODAY'S THOUGHT: "If at first you don't succeed, try again. Then quit. There's no use being a fool about it." —*W.C. Fields.*

OBSERVANCE/EVENT: Two great comedy stars were born today, Oliver Hardy in 1892 and Danny Kaye in 1913.

Graffiti

The supply of government is always greater than the demand!

JOKE: Hiring a new salesman, the boss warned him, "Now keep in mind that your salary is your business and no one else's."

"Certainly sir," replied the new employee, "and you don't have to worry. I'm as ashamed of it as you are."

January 19th

TODAY'S THOUGHT: "Man is the only animal that blushes — or needs to." —*Mark Twain*

OBSERVANCE/EVENT: One of the greatest of all Desilu productions debuted today in 1953, Desi Arnaz Jr.

Graffiti
Nuclear weapons are here to stay, but are we?

JOKE: Frick: I once knew a wealthy 80 year-old farmer who married a 20 year-old girl and couldn't keep his hands off her.
Frack: Did she object?
Frick: No, so he fired every one of them!

January 20th

TODAY'S THOUGHT: "Here's an interesting statistic. The world's population is growing by 170 people a minute, and still, the post office won't open another window." —*Jay Leno*

OBSERVANCE/EVENT: It is the dawning of the month or so of Aquarius and famous comedic Aquarians born today include George Burns, 1896 and *Laugh-In*'s Arte Johnson, who first got on the schtick in 1934.

Graffiti
Always finish what you sta...

JOKE:

Q: Why are all dumb blonde jokes one-liners?

A: *So men can understand them*

January 21st

TODAY'S THOUGHT: "We got a name for sushi in Georgia: bait." —*Blake Clark*

OBSERVANCE/EVENT: It's "National Hugging Day" so, as you read this, go ahead and squeeze the Charmin.

Graffiti
People who live beyond their means should act their wage.

JOKE: "I bought one of those records that you play while you sleep and in the morning you know a new language."
"How'd it work?"
"Not so good. The record stuck and now I stutter in Spanish."

January 22nd

TODAY'S THOUGHT: "Some people are afraid of heights. I'm afraid of widths." —*Steven Wright*

OBSERVANCE/EVENT: It's "Answer Your Cat's Question Day". Some of our favorite answers are:
Yes, dogs are incredibly gross;
No, I don't know why they don't make Mouse McNuggets;
and Alright already! I'll change the litter box!

Graffiti
Confucius say:
Woman who put detergent on top shelf jump for joy.

JOKE:

Q: What's more than a hundred feet tall and has four heads?

A: *Mount Rushmore*

January 23rd

TODAY'S THOUGHT: "TV is called a medium because it's rarely well done." —*Ernie Kovacs*

OBSERVANCE/EVENT: One of the great pioneers of TV comedy, Ernie Kovacs was born on this date in 1919.

Graffiti

Support bacteria! It's the only culture some people have.

JOKE: Three old geezers sitting on a porch watch a car speed by. The first geezer says, "That Chevy was going awfully fast."

A week later the second geezer says, "That wasn't a Chevy, it was a Caddy."

A month later the third geezer says, "If you two are gonna argue all the time, I'm leaving."

January 24th

TODAY'S THOUGHT: "I gave my cat a bath the other day...they love it. He sat there, he enjoyed it. It was fun for me. The fur would stick to my tongue but other than that..." —*Steve Martin*

OBSERVANCE/EVENT: Russia's funniest export since they sold all that nuclear waste to Eastern Europe as Pet Rockskis, Yakov Smirnoff was born in 1951.

Graffiti

A thief is a man of convictions.

JOKE: At a shopping mall, a little boy sat watching the down escalator as his mom paid for some merchandise. Taking his hand to leave after a few minutes, the little tyke piped up with, "Mommy, what do they do when the basement gets full of stairs?"

January 25th

TODAY'S THOUGHT: "All men make mistakes but husbands just find out about them sooner." *—Frank Coniff*

OBSERVANCE/EVENT: In 1915, Alexander Graham Bell placed the first transcontinental call to Thomas Watson in San Francisco. Later, just as Bell sat down to dinner, he got a call from a rival long distance company bugging him to switch.

Graffiti
Two Err Is Humin

JOKE: Did you hear the one about the guy who joined the Navy to see the world and spent four years on a submarine?

January 26th

TODAY'S THOUGHT: "Just be considerate, accept each other for what you are and don't point out that the hair he's losing on his head is now growing out of his nose — and ears." *—Peg Bundy (Married With Children)*

OBSERVANCE/EVENT: It's "Australia Day" so have a G'day, Mate.

Graffiti
Some "Open Minds" should be closed for repairs!

JOKE:

Q: What do you do if you find 50 lawyers up to their necks in concrete?

A: *Call for more concrete.*

January 27th

TODAY'S THOUGHT: "Have you noticed? Anyone going slower than you is an idiot, and anyone going faster than you is a moron." —*George Carlin*

OBSERVANCE/EVENT: Television was born in 1926 as inventor John Logie Baird first demonstrated the technology. The first television show? It was the face of an office boy seated in the downstairs laboratory. It was immediately followed by an infomercial about how to get rich quick in real estate.

Graffiti
Parking is such street sorrow!

JOKE: She's such a lousy cook you say grace after you eat!

January 28th

TODAY'S THOUGHT: "Like my old skleenball coach used to say, 'Find out what you don't do well and then don't do it.'" —*ALF*

OBSERVANCE/EVENT: Alphonso D'Abruzzo was born in 1936. He's better known as Hawkeye Pierce's alter-ego, Alan Alda.

Graffiti
A clean tie will always attract the soup of the day.

JOKE: The after-dinner speaker droned on and on as more and more people got up and left. Finally the room was empty save for one other guy.
Frustrated, the blowhard stopped his speech and asked why the man hadn't left like everyone else. To which the guy replied, "Because I'm the next speaker."

January 29th

TODAY'S THOUGHT: "It's always a good idea to keep a hip flask of Wild Turkey handy, as a stimulant, in case you see a snake, which you should also keep handy." —*W.C. Fields*

OBSERVANCE/EVENT: Officially, W.C. Fields was born in Philadelphia on this day in 1880 although it may have been several years earlier. Old William Claude always liked to keep everybody guessing.

Graffiti
A shotgun wedding is a case of wife or death.

JOKE: Did you hear the one about the 100 year-old man who went out with two nurses? Next time, they won't let him out without three.

January 30th

TODAY'S THOUGHT: "I really didn't say everything I said." —*Yogi Berra*

OBSERVANCE/EVENT: The world got its first look at *Laugh-In*'s Dick Martin's bippee on this day back in 1932, and not in beautiful downtown Burbank either, but in Detroit, Michigan.

Graffiti
Immorality is the morality of those who are having a better time than you are.

JOKE: Did you hear the one about the guy who was in the Stephen King Book Club? He cancelled his membership and the walls began to drip blood.

January 31st

TODAY'S THOUGHT: "Errol Flynn died on a seventy foot yacht with a seventeen year-old girl. Walter's always wanted to go like that but he's going to settle for a seventeen footer and a seventy year-old."
—*Mrs. Walter Cronkite*

OBSERVANCE/EVENT: "Hello, Dolly!" was said to Carol Channing as she was born on this day in 1923.

Graffiti

Horse sense is what keeps horses from betting on people.

JOKE:

Q: What's good for cold cuts?

A: *Frozen band-aids*

February 1st

TODAY'S THOUGHT: "I moved to Florida because you don't have to shovel water." —*James Randi*

OBSERVANCE/EVENT: Classic comedy troop members are part of today's birthday ensemble cast. Terry Jones of *Monty Python*, born in 1942 and Garrett Morris of the original *Saturday Night Live* Not Ready For Prime Time Players made his first "live" appearance in New Orleans in 1937.

Graffiti

Exercise daily. Eat Wisely. Die Anyway.

JOKE: Did you hear the one about the guy who wouldn't eat tongue sandwiches because they came out of an animal's mouth? He just had eggs for lunch.

February 2nd

TODAY'S THOUGHT: "To you I'm an atheist. To God I'm the loyal opposition." —*Woody Allen*

OBSERVANCE/EVENT: It's "Groundhog Day". Ancient legend has it that if the groundhog emerges and doesn't see his shadow, then you will be blessed with an early spring. If however, the groundhog sees his shadow because he's phoning it in from a beach in Aruba, watch out!

Graffiti

Fight air pollution — Inhale!

JOKE: My wife held her own special Groundhog Day celebration. She saw her shadow and signed up for six more weeks at the health club!

February 3rd

TODAY'S THOUGHT: "When a man says 'Honey, there are two minutes left in the football game,' that's the same amount of time as when his wife says 'Honey, I'll be dressed and ready in two minutes.'" *—Bobby Kelton*

OBSERVANCE/EVENT: Son of a Gun! Joey Bishop was born this day in 1918 and phone phunnyman Shelley Berman put the doctor on call in 1926.

Graffiti

Man who drink too much whiskey
could end up with wife as chaser.

JOKE: His stockbroker had a real track record. They tracked him through Bolivia. They tracked him through Argentina...

February 4th

TODAY'S THOUGHT: "I don't believe in astrology. I think horoscopes are crap, and all of us Libras feel the same way." *—Anonymous astronomy professor*

OBSERVANCE/EVENT: Two of the all-time biggest names in comedy share this birthday. David Brenner was born in 1945 and Dan Quayle in 1947.

Graffiti

Robin Hood's house had a Little John.

JOKE: And then there was the bodybuilder who had never been married. He could never find a woman who loved him as much as he did.

February 5th

TODAY'S THOUGHT: "I never realized how mediocre the world was until I got involved with some of its supposedly top people." —*Mason Williams*

OBSERVANCE/EVENT: Today is "Weatherman's Day", a time to remember that into each life, some rain must fall...especially on a weekend.

Graffiti

A bachelor is a man who never makes the same mistake once.

JOKE: "Hey Luigi," Ralph said as he sat in the barber chair, "my hair seems to be getting thinner and thinner. I think it's falling out. What can I use to keep it in?"

"I've got just the thing," smiled his old friend reaching under the counter. "Try one of my old cigar boxes."

February 6th

TODAY'S THOUGHT: "It's hard for me to get used to these changing times. I can remember when the air was clean and sex was dirty." —*George Burns*

OBSERVANCE/EVENT: Strange as it may seem, February not only is "National Snack Food Month", "National Cherry Month" and "Great American Pies Month", it's also "National Children's Dental Health Month". Go figure.

Graffiti

The meek may inherit the earth
but it's the enterprising who'll be collecting the estate tax.

JOKE:

Q: How do you get rid of a boomerang?

A: *Throw it down a one-way street.*

February 7th

TODAY'S THOUGHT: "A perfect vacation should be just long enough to make the boss miss you but not so long as to let him discover he can get along without you." —*Sanford Mims*

OBSERVANCE/EVENT: It's "National Hangover Awareness Day". Yesterday was Babe Ruth's birthday so that makes this the morning after "Babe's Night Out" when some of the all-time greatest hangovers known to man have been survived.

Graffiti
Bad dieters are usually poor losers!

JOKE: Did you hear about the cannibals who captured a group of politicians? They had to buy a crock pot to cook them.

February 8th

TODAY'S THOUGHT: "Economists report that a college education adds many thousands of dollars to a man's lifetime income which he then spends sending his son to college." —*Bill Vaughan*

OBSERVANCE/EVENT: Comedian Robert Klein was born on this date in 1942.

Graffiti
Have you hugged your porcupine today?

JOKE: He was so dumb he lost his job as proofreader in the M&M factory. He kept rejecting all the "W"s.

February 9th

TODAY'S THOUGHT: "A good rule of thumb is if you've made it to thirty-five and your job still requires you to wear a namc tag, you've probably made a serious vocational error." —*Dennis Miller*

OBSERVANCE/EVENT: Happy birthday to the Boeing 747 Jumbo Jet which first took flight on this date in 1969. It's odd to think that in today's fast-paced technological world, the airliners date from the 60's but then again, so does the airline food!

Graffiti
If flowers don't talk back to you, are they mums?

JOKE: "I hate golf. I hate golf. I hate golf."
"Nice shot."
"I love golf. I love golf. I love golf."

February 10th

TODAY'S THOUGHT: "When I was a kid, I had two friends, and they were imaginary. They would only play with each other." —*Rita Rudner*

OBSERVANCE/EVENT: The Great Schnozzola, Jimmy Durante, was born in New York City on this day in 1893.

Graffiti
Unzipped mail is immoral.

JOKE: Two women at a singles bar wearily watched a macho jock swagger by.
"I hear he thinks he's 'God's gift to women', " said the first.
"Well," said the second taking a sip of her drink,"I hope He kept the receipt."

February 11th

TODAY'S THOUGHT: "I am not a complete vegetarian. I only eat animals that have died in their sleep." —*George Carlin*

OBSERVANCE/EVENT: On this day in 1960, Jack Paar walked off the *Tonite Show* after an NBC censor had cut a mild "water closet" joke the night before.

Graffiti
Experience is what allows you to recognize a mistake when you make it again.

JOKE:

Q: What was the new home surgery kit called?

A: *Suture self*

February 12th

TODAY'S THOUGHT: "Lincoln showed that you can become somebody in Washington even if you're poor. George Washington proved that being rich doesn't hurt either." —*Milton Berle*

OBSERVANCE/EVENT: Sharing a birthday with Abe Lincoln (1809) is funnyman Arsenio Hall who was born on this date in 1955.

Graffiti
Hypochondriacs won't let well enough alone.

JOKE:

Q: What kind of music do mummies like best?

A: *Wrap*

February 13th

TODAY'S THOUGHT: "Human beings are the only creatures that allow their children to come back home." —*Bill Cosby*

OBSERVANCE/EVENT: It's "Get A Different Name Day". If your parents hung a monstrous moniker on you, today's your chance to enjoy any name you please. If, however, you sign your checks that way, your name will be "Mudd".

Graffiti

Hypochondriacs won't let well enough alone.

JOKE: Did you hear the one about the paranoid snake? He went to a psychiatrist because he had the feeling that behind his back all his friends were sticking their tongues out at him.

February 14th

TODAY'S THOUGHT: "Give me golf clubs, fresh air and a beautiful partner and you can keep my golf clubs and the fresh air." —*Jack Benny*

OBSERVANCE/EVENT: It's "Valentine's Day" and also the birthday of one of the all-time great laughmakers, Jack Benny, born in 1894.

Graffiti

Honesty is the best policy but insanity is a better defense!

JOKE: "You don't want to go to court with me, Baxley. My lawyer's smart and he knows the law!"
"Well, then you really don't want to go to court with me, Grimsbsy. My lawyer's sexy and she knows the judge!"

February 15th

TODAY'S THOUGHT: "When my son was born, I had this dream that one day he might grow up and be a Nobel Prize winner. But I also had another dream that he might grow up and have to say, 'Do you want fries with that?'" —*Robin Williams*

OBSERVANCE/EVENT: The "Second City", Chicago, added Harvey Korman to its cast in 1927.

> **Graffiti**
> *Whoever named it "necking" was a poor judge of anatomy.*

JOKE:

Q: What do you call identical twins who wear a hairpiece?

A: *Toupees in a pod*

February 16th

TODAY'S THOUGHT: "I can't stay — I'm leading a workshop on multiple personality disorders and it takes me forever to fill out the nametags."
—*Dr. Niles Crane (Frasier)*

OBSERVANCE/EVENT: Edgar Bergen got his first big laugh on this day in 1903. Throwing his voice sure scared the heck out of the obstetrician!

> **Graffiti**
> *Ignorance is when you don't know something and someone finds it out.*

JOKE:

Q: How do you make gold soup?

A: *You put in fourteen carrots.*

February 17th

TODAY'S THOUGHT: "It's amazing that the amount of news that happens in the world every day just exactly fits in the newspaper." *—Jerry Seinfeld*

OBSERVANCE/EVENT: It's "Vacuum Your Cat Day", a wacky day on which to Kirby your kitty. Just so you know, tomorrow is "Suture Your Shredded Skin Day".

Graffiti
An aquarium is a house of gill repute.

JOKE: Two birds are talking. One says to the other, "You look awful. Your feathers are frayed, your face looks like it was beaten to a pulp. What happened?"
"I got caught in a badminton game."

February 18th

TODAY'S THOUGHT: "If most accidents happen within five miles of home, why don't we move ten miles away?"
—Michael Davis

OBSERVANCE/EVENT: Believe it or not, on this date in 1930 Elm Farm Ollie became the first cow to fly in an airplane. No, they didn't show any moo-vies on the flight.

Graffiti
A polygon is a dead parrot.

JOKE: Did you hear about the unemployed schoolteacher? She has no class.

February 19th

TODAY'S THOUGHT: "You know what I hate? Indian givers...no, I take that back." *—Emo Philips*

OBSERVANCE/EVENT: It's "Temporary Insanity Day"! $*#%!*&@!!!!!

Graffiti
Surgeons make incision decisions.

JOKE: Army General: Do you have change for a dollar, soldier?
Private: I think so. Lemme see.
Army General: That's no way to talk to an officer. Let's try that again. Do you have change for a dollar?
Private: No, **sir**!

February 20th

TODAY'S THOUGHT: "I got an "A" in philosophy because I proved my professor didn't exist."
—Judy Teneta

OBSERVANCE/EVENT: John Glenn was the first to orbit the earth on this date in 1962, which reminds us: If athlete's get athlete's foot, what do astronauts get? Missile toe.

Graffiti
CIA agents are despised.

JOKE: I had a terrible dream last night. I dreamt I ate a giant marshmallow. When I woke up, my pillow was gone.

February 21st

TODAY'S THOUGHT: "If life was fair, Elvis would be alive and all the impersonators would be dead." *—Johnny Carson*

OBSERVANCE/EVENT: The woman who proclaimed that "any man who watches three consecutive football games should be declared legally dead" was born on this date in 1927, humorist Erma Bombeck.

Graffiti
What you seize is what you get!

JOKE: A salesman in San Juan wired his home office. "Stuck in Puerto Rico due to hurricane. Expect two week delay. Wire instructions."
His boss immediately wired back, "Begin vacation as of yesterday."

February 22nd

TODAY'S THOUGHT: "An earthquake is God grabbing the Earth and saying 'Cough.'" *—Richard Belzer*

OBSERVANCE/EVENT: It's George Washington's birthday...well, sort of. The date actually read February 11th when Washington was born but due to a major adjustment to the Gregorian calendar, his birthday was bumped back to the 22nd. Back then, leap years must have been murder!

Graffiti
Kamikazes do it once!

JOKE:

Q: What is it that you throw away the outside, cook the inside, eat the outside and throw away the inside?

A: *An ear of corn*

February 23rd

TODAY'S THOUGHT: "An economist is an expert who will know tomorrow why the things he predicted yesterday didn't happen today." *—Laurence J. Peter*

OBSERVANCE/EVENT: The man behind Mr. Magoo and that castaway captain of industry, Thurston Howell III, Jim Backus was born in 1913.

Graffiti
We are born naked, wet and hungry. Then things get worse.

JOKE: A guy runs up to a man in the street and says "Hey buddy, you seen a cop around here?"
"Why no, I haven't."
"Good. Then stick 'em up."

February 24rd

TODAY'S THOUGHT: "If a man is alone in a forest without a woman around, when he says something is it still wrong?" *—Bob Shulte, paraphrasing the age old "tree in a forest" question*

OBSERVANCE/EVENT: It's "National Obnoxious Day". Be sure to pay tribute to those possessed of a putrid personality. After all, they make the rest of us look a lot better.

Graffiti
A knob is a thing to adore.

JOKE:

Q: Why are computer viruses so dangerous?

A: *They could give you a terminal illness.*

February 25th

TODAY'S THOUGHT: "The reason there are two senators for each state is so that one can be the designated driver." —*Jay Leno*

OBSERVANCE/EVENT: It's "Go To The Opera Day" so call your local opera house and let them know you're "Carmen". This way, you'll end the day on a high note.

Graffiti
Historians are a thing of the past.

JOKE: Modern doctors are very sanitary. Did you ever notice they always wash their hands before touching your wallet?

February 26th

TODAY'S THOUGHT: "Anybody who goes to see a psychiatrist ought to have his head examined." —*Samuel Goldwyn*

OBSERVANCE/EVENT: "The Great One", Jackie Gleason, was born in 1916 and comic actor Tony Randall took his first bow in 1920.

Graffiti
What this country needs is a good no scent cigar.

JOKE: A guy goes to a lawyer and asks how much he charges.
"Two hundred dollars for three questions."
"That's a lot of money, isn't it?"
"Yep. What's your final question?"

February 27th

TODAY'S THOUGHT: "Why isn't 'phonetic' spelled the way it sounds?" —*The Atomic Cafe*

OBSERVANCE/EVENT: Liz Taylor was born on this day in 1932. Her nuptials have given the world such jokes as "Liz Taylor's been married so many times she's got a wash 'n' wear wedding gown" and "What do they throw at Liz Taylor's weddings? Minute Rice."

Graffiti
Don't put your foot down if you don't want it stepped on.

JOKE: The Answer is: despair
And the Question? What comes in handy when de tire goes flat?

February 28th

TODAY'S THOUGHT: "These detective series on TV always end at precisely the right moment — after the criminal is arrested and before the court turns him loose." —*Robert Orben*

OBSERVANCE/EVENT: The folks at *M*A*S*H* ended their eleven-year hitch on this date in 1983.

Graffiti
Man who put face in punch bowl get punch in nose.

JOKE: Did you hear the one about the tiny Chinese island that finally got mailboat service? All they get is junk mail.

February 29th

TODAY'S THOUGHT: "A race track is where windows clean people." —*Danny Thomas*

OBSERVANCE/EVENT: It's "Bachelor's Day", a day fittingly celebrated only in leap years. After all, those guys are having a pretty good time of it the other 1,460 days too.

Graffiti

Disintegrate Bigots!

JOKE: Two sharks happen to meet in the Gulf Stream. The first shark says, "Hey, who was that lady I saw you with last night?"

And the second shark says, "That was no lady, that was my dinner."

March 1st

TODAY'S THOUGHT: "If I only had a little humility, I'd be perfect." —*Ted Turner*

OBSERVANCE/EVENT: It's "National Pig Day", a day for those of the porcine persuasion to hog all the glory.

Graffiti
Pig farmers are disgruntled!

JOKE: "Oh, Mrs. Owens," gushed the baby-sitter visiting the maternity ward. "I can hardly believe it — *triplets* — how wonderful!"
"Yes it is, Sally," replied the proud mother. "Did you know that triplets only happen once in 4,657,842 times?"
"4,657,842 times?" Sally gasped. "When did you ever find time to clean the house?"

March 2nd

TODAY'S THOUGHT: "I'd rather go out with a perfect stranger than go on a blind date." —*Patti Putnicki*

OBSERVANCE/EVENT: It's "Peanut Butter Lover's Day" so whether you're dreamy for creamy or like to monkey with chunky, grind up those goobers and have the peanuttiest day that ever stuck to the roof of your mouth!

Graffiti
An editor makes a long story short.

JOKE: Frick: Hey Frack, how'd you get the broken arm?
Frack: I told someone I was shy.
Frick: How do you get a broken arm by telling someone you're shy?
Frack: It was my bookie and I was shy about two grand.

March 3rd

TODAY'S THOUGHT: "Military intelligence is a contradiction in terms." —*Groucho Marx*

OBSERVANCE/EVENT: It's "National Anthem Day", commemorating the anniversary of *The Star Spangled Banner* as our national anthem. The song narrowly beat out *America, The Beautiful, The Battle Hymn Of The Republic* and *Itsy-Bitsy Teeny-Weenie Yellow Polka-Dot Bikini.*

Graffiti
Is saltwater taffy seafood?

JOKE: He had a short career in politics. In fact, the only time he ever ran for anything he was considered a write-off candidate.

March 4th

TODAY'S THOUGHT: "My friend Larry is in jail now. He got twenty-five years for something he didn't do. He didn't run fast enough." —*Damon Wayans*

OBSERVANCE/EVENT: SCTV's Catherine O'Hara boosted the population of Toronto by one on this date in 1954 while another lady famous for monkeying around, Jane Goodall, was born in 1934.

Graffiti
Old soap bars never die, they just bathe away.

JOKE: A doctor called a patient and said, "Your check came back."
The patient replied, "So did my bursitis."

March 5th

TODAY'S THOUGHT: "If we do not succeed, then we run the risk of failure." *—Vice-President Dan Quayle*

OBSERVANCE/EVENT: March is "National Noodle Month" and "National Sauce Month". The pasta-bilities are endless!

Graffiti
Care enough to be apathetic.

JOKE: A guy tells his psychiatrist, "My wife thinks I have a problem because I like boxer shorts."
"That's no problem. I like boxer shorts myself."
"Really? With mustard or ketchup?"

March 6th

TODAY'S THOUGHT: "I envy people who drink. At least they know what to blame everything on." *—Oscar Levant*

OBSERVANCE/EVENT: It's "Meathead's" birthday. *All in the Family*'s Rob Reiner was born on this day in 1945.

Graffiti
Witches run spell-checkers.

JOKE:

Q: What happened to the employees at the struggling sardine factory?

A: *They were canned.*

March 7th

TODAY'S THOUGHT: "I don't make jokes. I just watch the government and report the facts." —*Will Rogers*

OBSERVANCE/EVENT: A big day for all you flakes out there...John Kellogg first served corn flakes in 1897.

Graffiti

If George Washington never told a lie, how'd he become president?

JOKE: Two fleas are standing on Fifth Avenue and 34th Street, planning to head up to New York's Central Park. One flea says to the other, "Shall we walk or take a dog?"

March 8th

TODAY'S THOUGHT: "You're not a kid anymore when you are obsessed with the thermostat."
—*Jeff Foxworthy*

OBSERVANCE/EVENT: This is "National Procrastination Week". Or was that last week?

Graffiti

In jail, you're here today and here tomorrow.

JOKE: Did you hear the one about the couple who wanted a civil wedding but decided on an open bar instead?

March 9th

TODAY'S THOUGHT: "The cost of living's going up and the chance of living's going down." —*Flip Wilson*

OBSERVANCE/EVENT: Flip your calendar to March 9th and then flip your lid. It's "Panic Day"! (Although it would seem much more appropriate on April 15th.)

Graffiti
Help Wanted: Psychic (You know where to apply.)

JOKE:

Q: What do you get if you cross a caterpillar with a parrot?

A: *A walkie-talkie*

March 10th

TODAY'S THOUGHT: "Nothing in life is 'fun for the whole family.'" —*Jerry Seinfeld*

OBSERVANCE/EVENT: The first person ever to "reach out and touch someone", Alexander Graham Bell did so today in 1876 with his invention of the telephone. In honor of the occasion, we bring you the following joke.

Graffiti
Wrong numbers are never busy.

JOKE: Alexander Graham Bell worked day and night trying to perfect his new invention. Jubilant, he made his first call to his assistant, Watson. A voice answered, "I'm not in right now, but if you'll leave your name..."

March 11th

TODAY'S THOUGHT:
"That money talks,
I'll not deny.
I heard it once,
It said: 'Goodbye.'" —*Richard Armour*

OBSERVANCE/EVENT: China's Ts'ai Lun invented paper on this day in 105 A.D. Bathroom readers everywhere owe him a debt of gratitude, in more ways than one.

Graffiti
Old accountants never die. They just lose their balance.

JOKE: March has some blustery winds. It was so windy the other day, a chicken laid the same egg three times!

March 12th

TODAY'S THOUGHT: "I don't think of myself as single. I'm romantically challenged." —*Stephanie Piro*

OBSERVANCE/EVENT: *Get Smart*'s 99 isn't quite that old yet. Barbara Feldon was born on this date in 1941.

Graffiti
"Let me mix that salad." — Caesar

JOKE: The wife of a prominent physician who was attending a convention in Las Vegas phoned the casino where she knew he'd be spending most of his time and asked to have him paged.
"Sorry ma'am," she was told. "The house does not make doctor calls."

March 13th

TODAY'S THOUGHT: "If you live to the age of a hundred you have it made, because very few people die past the age of a hundred." —*George Burns*

OBSERVANCE/EVENT: It's "Uncle Sam Day" marking the anniversary that everybody's richest uncle first made his appearance in *The New York Lantern* in 1852.

Graffiti
Bad coffee is grounds for divorce!

JOKE:

Q: How does Bugs Bunny stay in such great shape?
A: *Hareobics*

March 14th

TODAY'S THOUGHT: "The scientific theory I like best is that the rings of Saturn are composed entirely of lost airline luggage." —*Mark Russell*

OBSERVANCE/EVENT: It's "Moth er's Day" and that's not a typo. "Moth er's Day" is a celebration mounted by museums who get their collections out of moth balls and proudly display them. It's the one time of year the spotlight is on the moths rather than the other way around.

Graffiti
Old sailors never die, they just get a little dinghy.

JOKE: The Answer is: acoustic
And the Question? What do you use to shoot pool?

March 15th

TODAY'S THOUGHT: "Who invented the brush they leave next to the toilet? That thing hurts!" *—Andy Andrews*

OBSERVANCE/EVENT: It's "International Boss's Day Off", a time for bosses everywhere to just kick back and relax. If, by chance, you feel you're too busy to just take the day off, remember what happened to Caesar when he showed up on the job on this date.

Graffiti
Fortunetellers have a ball!

JOKE: Frick: Hey, how did you break your leg?
Frack: See those steps over there?
Frick: Yeah?
Frack: I didn't.

March 16th

TODAY'S THOUGHT: "If you watch a game, it's fun. If you play at it, it's recreation. If you work at it, it's golf." *—Bob Hope*

OBSERVANCE/EVENT: Another gift to the world from Newark, New Jersey — Jerry Lewis was born in 1925.

Graffiti
A toupee is a top secret.

JOKE: A Texas oilman was a constant bidder at an art auction and picked up three van Goghs, four Picassos, a Rembrandt and a half dozen Monets for a cool $25 million.
On leaving, he was overheard to say to his wife, "Okay — so that takes care of the Christmas cards. Now all we need are the gifts."

March 17th

TODAY'S THOUGHT: "My wife is an interior decorator. She wants to get rid of me because I clash with the drapes." —*Morey Amsterdam*

OBSERVANCE/EVENT: The town that can always claim the shortest St. Patrick's Day parade is Maryville, Missouri. They trim the procession annually to assure a new record. In 1991, the parade was 102 feet long and it's been shrinking ever since. Other towns must be green with envy!

Graffiti
He who buys a mobile home doesn't get a lot.

JOKE:

Q: What's green and stays out all night?

A: *Paddy O' Furniture*

March 18th

TODAY'S THOUGHT: "A lot of fellows nowadays have a B.A., M.D. or Ph.D. Unfortunately, they don't have a J.O.B." —*"Fats" Domino*

OBSERVANCE/EVENT: Bathroom Milestone — The Schick company caused quite a buzz when they marketed the world's first electric razor on this day in 1931.

Graffiti
The future isn't what it used to be.

JOKE:

Q: If a cannibal ate his mother's sister, what would you call him?

A: *An aunt-eater*

March 19th

TODAY'S THOUGHT: "My father was a successful businessman but he was ruined in the stock market crash... A big stockbroker jumped out the window and fell on his pushcart." —*Jackie Mason*

OBSERVANCE/EVENT: It was Ted Baxter's sign-off for the gang in the WJM newsroom as *The Mary Tyler Moore Show* aired its last episode on this date in 1977.

Graffiti

Parachutists jump for joy.

JOKE: A woman was driving her car and knitting at the same time. A motorcycle cop saw her, pulled alongside and said, "Pull over!"

She rolled down the window and replied, "No! Mittens."

March 20th

TODAY'S THOUGHT: "There's no limit to the amount of work a man can do provided, of course, that it isn't the work he's supposed to be doing at the moment." —*Robert Benchley*

OBSERVANCE/EVENT: Several of comedy's big guns got their shot at life on this day: Carl Reiner, 1922; Hal Linden, 1931; and Jerry Reed, 1937.

Graffiti

Where there's a will, there's a lawyer.

JOKE: There are just too many lawyers nowadays. Did you get a load of that new warning on a Magic 8 Ball? "Not advised for use as a home pregnancy test."

March 21st

TODAY'S THOUGHT: "We are given children to test us and make us more spiritual." —*George F. Will*

OBSERVANCE/EVENT: It's the "Future Birthday Of Captain James T. Kirk". Trekkies in Riverside, Iowa believe that the real Captain Kirk will boldly go where some man has obviously gone before and be born in the year 2228. Don't worry, there's still plenty of time to pick out a card.

Graffiti
Siamese twins make ends meet.

JOKE:

Q: What has a corncob pipe and a button nose and comes in the spring?

A: *Frosty the Puddle*

March 22nd

TODAY'S THOUGHT: "This town was so small they had a fashion show at Sears. No models, they just held open the catalog and the women would point." —*Joan Rivers*

OBSERVANCE/EVENT: It's "National Goof-Off Day", so just keep doing what you're doing.

Graffiti
A butterfly is a worm that turned.

JOKE: On Rodeo Drive in Beverly Hills, a sweet young thing walked into a boutique and called the clerk. "Excuse me, but I'd like to try on the dress in the window."

"Sorry, miss," the clerk replied. "You'll have to use the dressing room like everyone else."

March 23rd

TODAY'S THOUGHT: "Nepotism isn't all that bad as long as you keep it in the family." —*Winston Churchill*

OBSERVANCE/EVENT: It's "Near Miss Day". In 1989 an asteroid came within three hundred thousand miles of sending us the way of the dinosaurs. In space, that counts as a close shave.

Graffiti

Why don't fish have to wait an hour after they eat to go swimming again?

JOKE: Then there was the guy who bought a defective boomerang. No matter how hard he tried he couldn't return it.

March 24th

TODAY'S THOUGHT: "France is the only country where the money falls apart and you can't tear the toilet paper." —*Billy Wilder*

OBSERVANCE/EVENT: Comedic actor Norman Fell of *Three's Company* was born on this date in 1924.

Graffiti

Organic farming is tilling it like it is.

JOKE: Frick: Hey did you hear about Smithers?
Frack: No, what happened?
Frick: The old dog married an 18 year-old girl with an hourglass figure. He plans to spend his retirement playing in the sand.

March 25th

TODAY'S THOUGHT: "Money doesn't always bring happiness. People with $10 million aren't any happier than people with $9 million." —*Hobart Brown*

OBSERVANCE/EVENT: It's "Pecan Day" commemorating the planting by George Washington of pecan trees at Mt. Vernon on this day in 1775. Not surprisingly, to this day whenever people hear the word "Washington", they think of a bunch of nuts.

Graffiti
People with tact have less to retract.

JOKE:

Q: Why do bees hum?

A: *They can never remember the words.*

March 26th

TODAY'S THOUGHT: "Big sisters are the crabgrass in the lawn of life." —*Charles Shultz*

OBSERVANCE/EVENT: It's officially, or unofficially, "Make Up Your Own Holiday Day". Feel free to create your own special occasion. We sort of like "*Bathroom Joke Almanac* Appreciation Day".

Graffiti
Countries are making nuclear weapons like there's no tomorrow.

JOKE:

Q: What do you get when you cross a goat and an eel?

A: *An electric can opener*

March 27th

TODAY'S THOUGHT: "As a nation we are dedicated to keeping physically fit and parking as close to the stadium as possible." —*Bill Vaughn*

OBSERVANCE/EVENT: It's "National Joe Day", a day for people with unusual first names to get to be like regular Joes, or Joannes as the case may be.

Graffiti
Process servers put on the writs.

JOKE:
Q: What's a Republican turkey?
A: *One with two right wings*

March 28th

TODAY'S THOUGHT: A new survey says that 47% of people believe that astrology has some scientific proof. I don't believe in astrology because I'm an Aries and we are really skeptical." —*Conan O'Brien*

OBSERVANCE/EVENT: "Respect Your Cat Day" marks the anniversary of King Richard II's 1384 edict condemning the consumption of cats. That is no doubt how he came to be known as "King Richard the Kitty-Hearted".

Graffiti
A waist is a terrible thing to mind.

JOKE: A guy played cards with Siamese twins. When he was asked if he won, he replied, "Yes and no."

March 29th

TODAY'S THOUGHT: "The most important thing in acting is honesty. Once you've learned to fake that, you're in!" —*Samuel Goldwyn*

OBSERVANCE/EVENT: It's "Sing In The Shower Day" sponsored by *The Bathroom Joke Almanac.* Whether you're hardly able to croak a note or can carry an aria, this is the day to croon your tune in the shower.

Graffiti

The metric system doesn't measure up.

JOKE: "Doctor, we've got an emergency! My baby just swallowed all my tees."
"I'll be there at once."
"What should I do till you get here, Doc?"
"Practice your putting."

March 30th

TODAY'S THOUGHT: "She got her good looks from her father. He's a plastic surgeon." —*Groucho Marx*

OBSERVANCE/EVENT: It's "Doctors' Day" — and that reminds us of this burning question: Do doctors who treat people for amnesia make them pay in advance?

Graffiti

Ballet keeps you on your toes.

JOKE:

Q: What do you call a cow with no legs?
A: *Ground beef*

March 31st

TODAY'S THOUGHT: "When you come to the fork in the road, take it." —*Yogi Berra*

OBSERVANCE/EVENT: There'll be a hot time in the old town tonight as we celebrate "Bunsen Burner Day".

Graffiti

IRS: Income Removal Service

JOKE: "My, that's a beautiful diamond you have there," said one woman to the other.

"Yes, but it comes with a curse. This is the Klopman Diamond."

"Oh my!" said the wide-eyed admirer. "What's the curse?"

"Mr. Klopman."

April 1st

TODAY'S THOUGHT: "It's better to be looked over than overlooked." —*Mae West*

OBSERVANCE/EVENT: It's "April Fool's Day" so be on your guard for those merry pranksters and their classic practical jokes like putting Super Glue on the toilet seat...made you look — *Gotcha!*

Graffiti
Curl up with a hairdresser.

JOKE: A mama kangaroo pulled her little joey from her pouch, held him upside down by the tail and gave him several good whacks.
After the little kangaroo stopped crying she stuffed it back in her pouch and said, "That'll teach you not to eat crackers in bed!"

April 2nd

TODAY'S THOUGHT: "No matter how busy people are, they are never too busy to stop and talk about how busy they are." —*Bob Phillips*

OBSERVANCE/EVENT: The first United States Mint was established in Philadelphia on this date in 1792. It's also the only mint that was ever shut down by a strike. The workers there wanted to make less money.

Graffiti
Marshmallow peddling is a soft sell.

JOKE: The answer is: The Eiffel Tower. What's the question?
What would the Empire State Building look like after taxes?

April 3rd

TODAY'S THOUGHT: "Fishing is a delusion entirely surrounded by liars in old clothes." *—Don Marquis*

OBSERVANCE/EVENT: It's "Don't Go To Work Unless It's Fun Day", actually part of a fortnight of fun and frolic including "Discover Your Boss Has No Sense Of Humor Day" and "Don't Bother Showing Up At The Unemployment Office, They're Never Going To Buy It Day".

Graffiti

Good accountants keep you in the black and the IRS in the dark.

JOKE: And then there was the guy who got a job at the circus as a human cannonball. He was hired and fired the same night.

April 4th

TODAY'S THOUGHT: "Never learn to do anything: if you don't learn, you'll always find someone else to do it for you." *—Mark Twain*

OBSERVANCE/EVENT: It's "Dog Appreciation Month" so pack up your pooper-scooper and give Fido a new leash on life as you take your best friend for a walk.

Graffiti

Bad spellers of the world, untie!

JOKE: At Sunday school, the teacher was leading the class in a discussion of what Noah might have done to pass time on the ark.

"I think he went fishing," said one little girl.

The little boy sitting alongside gave her a look and piped up, "What...with only two worms?"

April 5th

TODAY'S THOUGHT: "Adults are always asking little kids what they want to be when they grow up — 'cause they're looking for ideas." *—Paula Poundstone*

OBSERVANCE/EVENT: It's "Lady Luck Day" so lay your cards on the table and be thankful when Dame Fortune smiles upon you.

Graffiti
Whistler's mother was off her rocker.

JOKE:

Q: How do you telephone a police dog?

A: *Dial K911*

April 6th

TODAY'S THOUGHT: "If you don't want to work, you have to work to earn enough money so that you don't have to work." *—Ogden Nash*

OBSERVANCE/EVENT: The North Pole was discovered in 1909 by Admiral Peary. Well, actually, it was discovered by a member of his expedition, Matthew Henson. Well, actually the North *geographic* Pole was discovered by Henson. The North Pole itself was discovered by one of Henson's sled dogs who had waited a long time between trees.

Graffiti
Down with everything that's up!

JOKE: Did you hear the one about the tiddlywink champ who had to retire? He sprained his wink finger.

April 7th

TODAY'S THOUGHT: "I eat so much pizza that when I was away for two weeks, Domino's sent me a get-well card. I was gone for a month and they put my picture on the pizza boxes. It read 'Have you seen this man...?'" *—Doug Graham*

OBSERVANCE/EVENT: It's "No Housework Day". Skip the dishes, vacuuming, dusting and all that. Do nothing. As a matter of fact, we suggest you start out the day by going back to bed.

Graffiti

Soldiers do it fatigued.

JOKE: Did you hear the one about the sheep rustler who broke out of jail and is now on the lamb?

April 8th

TODAY'S THOUGHT: "I never hated a man enough to give him the diamonds back." *—Zsa Zsa Gabor*

OBSERVANCE/EVENT: Comedian Shecky Greene was born on this date in 1925.

Graffiti

Happiness is having a scratch for every itch.

JOKE: Two convicts, Muggsy and Bugsy, were about to be executed. The warden says to Muggsy, "Do you have a last request?"

The condemned man says, "Yes. I'd like to hear *Achy Breaky Heart* one last time."

The Warden says to Bugsy, "How about you? Any last request?"

And Bugsy says, "Yeah. Kill me first."

April 9th

TODAY'S THOUGHT: "The difference between divorce and legal separation is that legal separation gives a husband time to hide his money." —*Johnny Carson*

OBSERVANCE/EVENT: It's "Longest Word Day" marking the publication of a word of 207,000 letters in a scientific journal. Actually it was really a string of over 50,000 four-letter words spewed out by a scientist who had a Bunsen burner fall in his lap.

Graffiti
Celibacy is not hereditary!

JOKE: Did you hear the one about the guy who drank 6 cups of coffee and 6 cups of decaf?
He stayed up half the night.

April 10th

TODAY'S THOUGHT: "I don't believe in an afterlife, although I am bringing a change of underwear."
—*Woody Allen*

OBSERVANCE/EVENT: The first professional golf tournament ever held in the United States was played at the Siwanoy Golf Course in Bronxville, New York in 1916. Accordingly, *The Bathroom Joke Almanac* pronounces this "Golf Widow Day".

Graffiti
Jack and Jill are over the hill.

JOKE: Sign on barbershop: *We Give $3 Haircuts.*
Sign on barbershop across the street: *We Repair $3 Haircuts.*

April 11th

TODAY'S THOUGHT: "'Buffet' is a French term. It means get up and get it yourself." —*Greg Ray*

OBSERVANCE/EVENT: April is "National Humor Month". Keep that in mind while filling out your tax forms.

Graffiti

Life is like a shower —
a wrong turn can leave you in hot water.

JOKE: A doctor says to his patient, "I have some bad news and some worse news. The bad news is that you have only 24 hours to live."
The patient says, "Oh, no, what could possibly be worse than that?"
"I forgot to tell you yesterday."

April 12th

TODAY'S THOUGHT: "Insanity is hereditary; you can get it from your children." —*Sam Levenson*

OBSERVANCE/EVENT: On this date in 1934, observers on Mt. Washington, New Hampshire registered gusts of 231 mph, the highest natural wind gusts ever recorded outside of a presidential election campaign.

Graffiti

If you don't have a leg to stand on, it's best not to kick.

JOKE:
Q: What do you get if you cross an owl and a goat?
A: *A hootenanny*

April 13th

TODAY'S THOUGHT: "Until Eve arrived, this was a man's world." —*Anonymous*

OBSERVANCE/EVENT: It's "National Fresh Celery Month". It's crunch time so feel free to stalk your favorite vegetable.

Graffiti
Get even. Live long enough to be a burden to your kids.

JOKE: Two old codgers were reminiscing. "My first girlfriend was named Mary Katherine Agnes Colleen Patricia Marion Margaret Kathleen O'Shaunessey — I carved her name in a tree."
"Whatever happened?" asked his friend.
"The tree fell on me."

April 14th

TODAY'S THOUGHT: "Never eat more than you can lift." —*Miss Piggy*

OBSERVANCE/EVENT: On this day in 1910, President Taft began the sports tradition of throwing out the first baseball of the season. Not that it has anything to do with the game, but we discovered that the 325-pound Taft once got stuck in the White House bathtub and had to be helped out by four men. Just thought you'd like to know.

Graffiti
Parrots speak in polly-syllables.

JOKE:

Q: What's the penalty for bigamy?

A: *Two mothers-in-law*

April 15th

TODAY'S THOUGHT: "There is one difference between a tax collector and a taxidermist — the taxidermist leaves the hide." —*Mortimer Caplan*

OBSERVANCE/EVENT: The Titanic went down on this date in 1912 and since the federal income tax began in 1913, people have been getting a sinking feeling on this day ever since.

Graffiti

The Ides Of Taxes are upon you.

JOKE: A beggar knocked on a rich guy's door at 2 a.m. "How dare you wake me up at this time in the morning!" yelled the rich guy.
The beggar replied, "Hey, I don't tell you how to run your business so don't tell me how to run mine."

April 16th

TODAY'S THOUGHT: "I thought I could do my own small part to save the planet by becoming a vegetarian. Actually, I did it not so much because I love animals but because I hate plants. I still like to hunt though. In fact, I've found that plants are a lot easier than animals to sneak up on." —*A. Whitney Brown*

OBSERVANCE/EVENT: The long-running radio comedy *Fibber McGee and Molly* premiered in 1935.

Graffiti

Enjoy Daylight Savings Time —
it'll probably be the only thing you save all year!

JOKE: Then there was the dyslexic agnostic who had insomnia. He stayed up all night wondering if there really was a Dog.

April 17th

TODAY'S THOUGHT: "I know there are people in the world who do not love their fellow human beings. I hate people like that." —*Tom Lehrer*

OBSERVANCE/EVENT: Today celebrates a little horse sense: The first horse was brought to America in 1629 and the classic sports car, the Mustang, was introduced in 1964.

Graffiti
Love is blind but marriage is a real eye opener!

JOKE:

Q: Where do they imprison the man who was convicted of assault and battery?

A: *In a dry cell*

April 18th

TODAY'S THOUGHT: "Always forgive your enemies but never forget their names." —*Robert Kennedy*

OBSERVANCE/EVENT: It's "Pet Owner Independence Day", a day when pet owners are supposed to stay home and send their pampered pets out to do their jobs. If your job entails shedding, coughing up fur balls or staining carpets it might work out for you, otherwise it's probably not a valid excuse for your boss unless, of course, you bring a note from your veterinarian.

Graffiti
Never slap a guy in the face who is chewing tobacco.

JOKE: Did you hear the one about the male snake charmer who married a female undertaker? Their bath towels read "Hiss" and "Hearse".

April 19th

TODAY'S THOUGHT: "Familiarity breeds contempt... and children." —*Mark Twain*

OBSERVANCE/EVENT: "Would you believe" that Don Adams was born this day in 1927?

Graffiti

Old mufflers never die, they just get exhausted.

JOKE: A guy comes into a doctor's office with two bright red ears.
"Doc, this is really dumb. I was at the ironing board and the phone rang and without thinking I picked up the iron instead of the phone."
"Ouch! That's gotta hurt," said the doctor. "But what happened to the other ear?"
"Oh, that. They called back."

April 20th

TODAY'S THOUGHT: "When I was a boy, my mother wore a mood ring. Whenever she was in a good mood it would turn blue. Whenever she was in a bad mood it left a big red mark in the middle of my forehead." —*Jeff Shaw*

OBSERVANCE/EVENT: It's "National Recycling Month" so remember, when you read an old joke, we're just doing our part.

Graffiti

It's not the minutes spent at the table that expand your waistline... it's the seconds.

JOKE: The answer is Camelot...and the question? Where does a camel park?

April 21st

TODAY'S THOUGHT: "Well, enough about me. Let's talk about you. What do you think of me?" —*Bette Midler*

OBSERVANCE/EVENT: It's "Change Your Toothbrush Day" brought to you by the publishers of this book. If you bristle at the thought of disposing of a perfectly good toothbrush, just remember that dental experts agree it's easier to change your toothbrush than change your teeth.

Graffiti
A cat may have nine lives but a frog croaks every night.

JOKE: What's the difference between a hunter and a fisherman?
A hunter lies in wait; a fisherman waits and lies.

April 22nd

TODAY'S THOUGHT: "A lot of couples shower together. It's supposed to be romantic and sensual. Truth? It's not all it's cracked up to be. Because one of you is not getting water. One of you, therefore, is not taking a shower." —*Paul Reiser*

OBSERVANCE/EVENT: It's "Be Careful What You Say Day". 'Nuff said.

Graffiti
Marriage — a knot tied by a minister, untied by a lawyer.

JOKE:

Q: How does a scared calf behave?

A: *Cow-ardly*

April 23rd

TODAY'S THOUGHT: "Drinking makes such fools of people, and people are such fools to begin with that it's compounding a felony." —*Robert Benchley*

OBSERVANCE/EVENT: *The Bathroom Joke Almanac*'s favorite form of social protest, the sit-in, was perfected on this date in 1968 as demonstrators closed down Columbia University.

Graffiti

Censors stick their "nos" into other people's business.

JOKE: Receptionist: There's a man in the waiting room who thinks he's invisible.
Psychiatrist: Tell him I can't see him right now.

April 24th

TODAY'S THOUGHT: "The four stages of man are infancy, childhood, adolescence and obsolescence." —*Art Linkletter*

OBSERVANCE/EVENT: Celebrate "Ambivalence Day"... or not.

Graffiti

No matter how much you hate reading prose —
it could be verse.

JOKE: A woman called the town paper to place an obituary notice for her husband. She wanted it to read "Farnsworth died."
The sales clerk said, "Is that all? You can add three more words for the same price, lady."
The woman added, "Cadillac for sale."

April 25th

TODAY'S THOUGHT: "Sports is the only entertainment where, no matter how many times you go back, you never know the ending." —*Neil Simon*

OBSERVANCE/EVENT: In England, April 25th is Cuckoo Day. In Washington D.C., every day is Cuckoo Day.

Graffiti
Two wrongs might make a riot.

JOKE: A woman was doing some spring cleaning when she came across an old box with a shoe repair claim ticket in it. She brought it to the shoe repair shop and said to the owner, "Look at this. I brought my shoes here to be re-soled 10 years ago and forgot about it." The owner replied, "They'll be ready next Tuesday."

April 26th

TODAY'S THOUGHT: "Mary had a little lamb. The doctor fainted." —*Anonymous*

OBSERVANCE/EVENT: It's "Hug An Australian Day". Give them a squeeze to please to promote continued friendly relations with our mates Down Under. By the way, bring this book with you as proof that this isn't some sort of cheesy Yank come-on.

Graffiti
If life is a waste of time, and time is a waste of life, then let's all get wasted together and have the time of our lives.

JOKE: Did you hear the one about the guy who read the *Cliff's Notes* version of *Walden*? It wasn't very "Thoreau".

April 27th

TODAY'S THOUGHT: "It doesn't make sense. You're flying 500 mph, 30,000 feet in the air and the pilot tells you to feel free to roam around the plane. But when you're on the ground taxiing to the gate at one mph, he tells you to remain seated for your own safety." *—Elayne Boosler*

OBSERVANCE/EVENT: The fourth Saturday in April brings the World Championship Cow Chip Throw to Beaver, Oklahoma so if you're into bull slinging, limber up and go for the gold.

Graffiti

Of all the the things I've lost, I miss my mind the most.

JOKE: Did you hear the one about the glassblower who inhaled? He got a pane in the stomach.

April 28th

TODAY'S THOUGHT: "It's all right letting yourself go as long as you can let yourself back." *—Mick Jagger*

OBSERVANCE/EVENT: It's "Kiss-Your-Mate Day". Kiss your mate to show them how much you care. You'll probably get a kiss right back — unless you're in Australia in which case kissing your "mate" will get you a punch in the kisser.

Graffiti

Confucius say: Man with unchecked parachute will jump to conclusion.

JOKE: Strip poker is the only game in the world where the more you lose, the more you have to show for it.

April 29th

TODAY'S THOUGHT: "The biggest waste of water in the country by far. You spend a pint and flush two gallons." —*Duke of Edinburgh*

OBSERVANCE/EVENT: Crack a smile as it's "Moment of Laughter Day". It's also the birthday of someone whose given us many of those moments, Jerry Seinfeld (1954).

Graffiti
Anarchy rules!

JOKE:

Q: What do you get when you cross a teacher with a vampire?

A: *Lots of blood tests*

April 30th

TODAY'S THOUGHT: "Hope is the feeling you have that the feeling you have isn't permanent." —*Jean Kerr*

OBSERVANCE/EVENT: It's "National Honesty Day"...really. Would we lie to you?

Graffiti
If at first you don't succeed — cheat!

JOKE: A man goes to a psychiatrist's office, takes out a pouch of pipe tobacco and sticks it in his ear. Seeing this, the psychiatrist says, "It seems you've come to the right place. How can I help you?"
The guy replies, "You can give me a light."

May 1st

TODAY'S THOUGHT: "Old age is the time when men pay more attention to the food than they do to the waitress." —*Albert Fletcher*

OBSERVANCE/EVENT: May is "Correct Posture Month" and *The Bathroom Joke Almanac* is just what the doctor ordered for a slumping slouch. All month long, whenever you're sitting in the bathroom, close the book and place it on your head.

Graffiti

Why do they call it a "Political Forum" when most of us are againstum?

JOKE: Did you hear the one about the book on levitation? You just can't put it down.

May 2nd

TODAY'S THOUGHT: "There's a pizza place near where I live that sells only slices. In the back, you can see a guy tossing a triangle in the air." —*Steven Wright*

OBSERVANCE/EVENT: You'll find a lot of crabs at the Jersey Shore but the only one who has his own day is Martin Z. Mollusk, Ocean City's official hermit crab. If he sees his shadow on the first Thursday in May, summer comes a week early and that means some tourist will step on him a week sooner.

Graffiti

If love is blind, why is lingerie so popular?

JOKE: "Waiter, there's a fly in my soup."
"Could be. The chef used to be a tailor."

May 3rd

TODAY'S THOUGHT: "Guidelines for bureaucrats: (1) When in charge, ponder. (2) When in trouble, delegate. (3) When in doubt, mumble."
—James H. Boren

OBSERVANCE/EVENT: It's "Lumpy Rug Day". Not only is this event celebrated coast-to-coast, it's observed wall-to-wall.

Graffiti
An elephant never forgets, but what does he have to remember?

JOKE:

Q: What did the beaver say to the tree?
A: *It's been nice gnawing you.*

May 4th

TODAY'S THOUGHT: "What they put women through today when they're having a baby. They don't want to medicate them, as compared to previous generations. When my mom had me, she had so much medication she didn't wake up till I was seven." *—Dennis Wolfberg*

OBSERVANCE/EVENT: It's "Naked Day" — okay if you're in the bathroom but we're not responsible otherwise.

Graffiti
My mother was the travel agent for guilt trips.

JOKE: Holdup Man: Your money or your life!
Victim: Go ahead and take my life. I'm gonna need my money for my old age.

May 5th

TODAY'S THOUGHT: "I saw an announcement at the end of a TV show the other night. It said "If you'd like a copy of this program and were too lazy, inept or stupid to tape it yourself, send $29.95..." *—Burl Wood*

OBSERVANCE/EVENT: It's "Carpet Care Improvement Week". Don't be steamed because your puppy gave you a deep pile carpet, but we do advise that you work up a lather.

Graffiti

You can lead a man to water
but you can't make him put the seat back down.

JOKE: And then there was the would-be entrepreneur who was duped into buying hundreds of cases of Cheerios. He was told they were bagel seeds.

May 6th

TODAY'S THOUGHT: "I went to art school but just for about three weeks. I got kicked out for tracing." *—Margaret Smith*

OBSERVANCE/EVENT: "National Hoagie Day" honors the greatest culinary creation ever to come out of Philadelphia. We can all show our respect for this classic American meal today by eschewing terms such as "Sub", "Hero", "Poor Boy" and "Grinder" and ordering up a real South Philly Hoagie.

Graffiti

When you jump to conclusions, there is never a safety net.

JOKE: Two eagles see a jet streak by.
Eagle 1: That bird was sure in a hurry.
Eagle 2: You'd be in a hurry too if your tail was on fire!

May 7th

TODAY'S THOUGHT: "You can fool too many of the people too much of the time." *—James Thurber*

OBSERVANCE/EVENT: May is "Fungal Infection Awareness Month". 'Nuff said.

Graffiti
A school is a mental institution.

JOKE: The expectant father had a furrowed brow.
"What's the matter?" asked the other man in the maternity ward waiting room.
"My wife read *Tale of Two Cities* and had twins. The next year she read *The Three Musketeers* and had triplets," replied the nervous father.
"So?"
"She just finished *Birth of a Nation*!"

May 8th

TODAY'S THOUGHT: "If you women knew what we were thinking, you'd never stop slapping us." *—Larry Miller*

OBSERVANCE/EVENT: It's"No Socks Day", a casual dress day for your feet. Every May 8th, people across the country choose to kick up their heels and step out without any socks. That's why May 9th is now "National Blister Day".

Graffiti
Computer mating is dater-processing.

JOKE:

Q: Why did the chicken cross the highway?

A: *To lay it on the line*

May 9th

TODAY'S THOUGHT: "Did you ever feel like the whole world was a tuxedo and you were a pair of brown shoes?" —*George Gobel*

OBSERVANCE/EVENT: The wheel was invented in 50,000 B.C. but the button hole wasn't invented until 1247 so, until then, all those little wheels they sewed on clothes didn't work. It's "Hooray For Buttons Day". Here's hoping you have all of yours.

Graffiti
Life begins when you get one.

JOKE:

Q: What do you call an animal with four legs and one arm?

A: *A pit bull.*

May 10th

TODAY'S THOUGHT: "An economic downturn is when they don't have money. A recession is when you don't have money. A depression is when I don't have money." —*Sanford Mims*

OBSERVANCE/EVENT: *Laugh-In*'s Gary Owens, the voice of Beautiful Downtown Burbank, made his birth announcement on this day in 1936.

Graffiti
Never repeat yourself. Never.

JOKE: Not all fairy tales begin with "Once upon a time." Some begin with "If I'm elected..."

May 11th

TODAY'S THOUGHT: "A yuppie is someone who believes it's courageous to eat in a restaurant that hasn't been reviewed yet." —*Mort Sahl*

OBSERVANCE/EVENT: Satirist and 50's counterculture icon Mort Sahl was born on this day in 1927.

Graffiti
If you've lost your memory, forget about it.

JOKE:

Q: What do you get when you cross a rooster with another rooster?

A: *Two very cross roosters*

May 12th

TODAY'S THOUGHT: "Men will now get up and walk with the baby in the middle of the night, change its diapers and give it a bottle but in their heart of hearts they still think they shouldn't have to." —*Rita Rudner*

OBSERVANCE/EVENT: George Carlin was born on this day in 1937. It was a difficult birth. In fact, his mother used all seven words that you can't say on TV.

Graffiti
Oceanography is a study in depth.

JOKE: Did you hear the one about the woman who was going to get a facelift? When she found out the price she let the whole thing drop.

May 13th

TODAY'S THOUGHT: "I don't think anybody should write his autobiography until after he's dead." —*Samuel Goldwyn*

OBSERVANCE/EVENT: It's "National Receptionist Day", a day to recognize the great contributions receptionists make to business. The organizers say that flowers and a champagne toast are in order. Why not have your receptionist call and order some up?

Graffiti
He who laughs, lasts.

JOKE: The Amazing Kreskin once had a girlfriend who broke off with him. All he wanted was her mind.

May 14th

TODAY'S THOUGHT: "If you don't go to other people's funerals, they won't go to yours." —*Clarence Day*

OBSERVANCE/EVENT: The "Stars And Stripes Forever Day" is the anniversary of the first public performance of John Philip Sousa's famous march in 1897. Straight-laced Philadelphians and President William McKinley alike got down to the sound and boogied the night away.

Graffiti
A gossip is the knife of the party.

JOKE: The answer is: deduce
And the question? What is de lowest card in de deck?

May 15th

TODAY'S THOUGHT: "A man who has never gone to school may steal from a freight car but if he has a university education, he may steal from the whole railroad." —*Theodore Roosevelt*

OBSERVANCE/EVENT: It's "National Employee Health and Fitness Day", an occasion to focus on the importance of fitness and healthy lifestyles at the worksite. We also hear that exercise kills germs. But how do you get the little buggers to exercise?

Graffiti

Recycling: The return trip of a bike race.

JOKE: Woman: Oh, your grandchildren are so precious. How old are they?
Grandma: Well, the doctor is four and the lawyer is six.

May 16th

TODAY'S THOUGHT: "Can you believe a candidate dropped out of the race because of a lack of campaign funds? Any politician who stops spending just because he's out of money doesn't belong in Washington." —*Kevin Nealon*

OBSERVANCE/EVENT: May is "National Mime Month" but mum's the word.

Graffiti

Multiple births are a midwife crisis.

JOKE: Frick: My cousin bought a car for only $100.
Frack: Only $100? I can't get over it!
Frick: Neither can he. He's always under it.

May 17th

TODAY'S THOUGHT: "My father invented the burglar alarm which, unfortunately, was stolen from him."
—Victor Borge

OBSERVANCE/EVENT: The guy who made a fortune off other people's home movies, Bob Saget, was born in Philadelphia on this day in 1956.

Graffiti
I left my heart in San Francisco
but everything else went in Vegas!

JOKE:

Q: If a Czar's wife is a Czarina, what would you call their children?

A: *Czardines*

May 18th

TODAY'S THOUGHT: "Stay humble. Always answer the phone — no matter who else is in the car."
—Jack Lemmon

OBSERVANCE/EVENT: It's "Visit Your Relatives Day". Renew family bonds, catch up on how things are going. Visit your relatives before they visit you.

Graffiti
It's not the bulls or the bears that get you
in the stock market...it's the bum steers.

JOKE: The law presumes a man innocent until proven guilty. After that, if he has any money left, his lawyer continues the presumption.

May 19th

TODAY'S THOUGHT: "You've got to be very careful if you don't know where you're going, because you might not get there." —*Yogi Berra*

OBSERVANCE/EVENT: The third week in May is designated "National Senior Smile Week" so be sure to greet those senior smiles in kind whether you see them on the street, at the office or in a glass.

Graffiti
Procrastinators have wait problems.

JOKE:

Q: What happened when the elephant sat on the grape?

A: *It let out a little wine.*

May 20th

TODAY'S THOUGHT: "The reason it's called 'golf' is that all the other four-letter words were taken." —*Leslie Nielsen*

OBSERVANCE/EVENT: That Toddlin' Town gained one more future toddler as "Lonesome" George Gobel was born in Chicago on this day in 1919.

Graffiti
Easy Street is a blind alley.

JOKE:

Q: What happened after the termites ate the Chinese restaurant?

A: *An hour later, they ate the building next door.*

May 21st

TODAY'S THOUGHT: "Men aren't attracted to me by my mind. They're attracted to me by what I don't mind." *—Gypsy Rose Lee*

OBSERVANCE/EVENT: To: All interested parties
From: The Bathroom Joke Almanac
Subject: National Memo Day
If you deal daily with a mountain of moronic memos, this is your day to post your own memo concerning the fact that there are too many memos.

Graffiti
Old basketball players never die. They just dribble away.

JOKE: Then there was the guy who worked at a fire hydrant plant but quit after six months because he could never park near the place.

May 22nd

TODAY'S THOUGHT: "Government investigations have always contributed more to our amusement than they have to our knowledge." *—Will Rogers*

OBSERVANCE/EVENT: Note a big day in bathroom history as Dr. Sheffield invented the toothpaste tube in 1892. It's also the anniversary of the day those immortal words, "Please squeeze from the bottom," were first uttered.

Graffiti
Just when you start winning the rat race,
you run into faster rats.

JOKE: Did you hear the one about the guy who, after only one karate lesson, can now break a board with his cast?

May 23rd

TODAY'S THOUGHT: "I have a microwave fireplace. You can lay down in front of the fire all night in eight minutes." —*Steven Wright*

OBSERVANCE/EVENT: It's "Don't Rob A Bank Day". In case you've been considering it, remember the fate of Bonnie and Clyde.

Graffiti
Dermatologists make rash judgments!

JOKE:

Q: How many lawyers does it take to screw in a lightbulb?

A: *How many can you afford?*

May 24th

TODAY'S THOUGHT: "The man who sees the consistency in things is a wit; the man who sees the inconsistencies in things is a humorist."
—*G.K. Chesterton*

OBSERVANCE/EVENT: *M*A*S*H*'s Gary Burghoff met his first doctor in 1934 and the man behind Miss Piggy, Frank Oz, was born in 1944.

Graffiti
A digital clock doesn't run clockwise.

JOKE: A friend of mine went to his doctor because he heard ringing in his head. The doctor gave him an unlisted ear.

May 25th

TODAY'S THOUGHT: "I don't deserve this but then I have arthritis and I don't deserve that either." *—Jack Benny, accepting an award*

OBSERVANCE/EVENT: It's "National Tap Dance Day" celebrated on the birthday of Bill Bojangles Robinson. If you can't celebrate with a tap dance, head for a tap room.

> **Graffiti**
> *If one synchronized swimmer drowns, do the rest have to drown too?*

JOKE: She's so old that when she went to school, they didn't have history yet.

May 26th

TODAY'S THOUGHT: "We experience moments absolutely free from worry. These brief respites are called panic." *—Colleen Hightower*

OBSERVANCE/EVENT: It's "Put Up Your Dukes Day" observed on John Wayne's birthday so put up or shut up, pilgrim.

> **Graffiti**
> *The girl who is easy to get may be hard to take.*

JOKE: "Senator — to show my appreciation I'd like to give you a $60,000 Mercedes from my dealership."
"I can't accept that, man, it would be bribery!"
"I could arrange to sell you the car for $50."
"In that case, I'll take two!"

May 27th

TODAY'S THOUGHT: "Some tortures are physical and some are mental but the one that's both is dental." —*Ogden Nash*

OBSERVANCE/EVENT: In 1919, Charles Strite patented the pop-up toaster, an invention that no doubt has made a lot of bread.

Graffiti
If you want a stable life, marry a horse.

JOKE:

Q: What's the opposite of Progress?

A: *Congress*

May 28th

TODAY'S THOUGHT: "The reason lightning doesn't strike twice in the same place is that the same place isn't there the second time." —*Willie Tyler*

OBSERVANCE/EVENT: It's "Spy Novels Are Splendid Day", on the birthday of author Ian Fleming whose words were his Bond...James Bond.

Graffiti
If God expected us to be brave, why did he give us legs?

JOKE: Two men are sitting at a bar when one glances at the TV set and says, "You know, I got a TV just like that for my mother-in-law."
The guy next to him puts down his glass and says wistfully, "Gee, I'd love to make a deal like that."

May 29th

TODAY'S THOUGHT: "The shortest recorded period of time lies between the minute you put some money away for a rainy day and the unexpected arrival of rain." *—Jane Bryant Quinn*

OBSERVANCE/EVENT: Comedian Bob Hope started out on the road to life on this day in 1903.

Graffiti

24 hours in a day...24 beers in a case... coincidence?

JOKE: "He's filthy rich. He flies his own Cessna."
"A lot of people fly their own Cessna."
"In the living room?"

May 30th

TODAY'S THOUGHT: "If there's anyone listening to whom I owe money, I'm prepared to forget it if you are." *—Errol Flynn*

OBSERVANCE/EVENT: The first automobile accident occurred on this date in New York City in 1898. Also, the first personal injury lawyer chased the first ambulance.

Graffiti

To cure that listless feeling, write a list.

JOKE: Diner: I think I'll have what that man over there is having.
Waiter: Alright, sir. But I don't think he's going to be too happy about it.

May 31st

TODAY'S THOUGHT: "If I accept the anti-nude morality, I must be ashamed of my own body. But where can I go without it?" —*Alan Sherman*

OBSERVANCE/EVENT: It's "Take This Job And Shove It Day", the birthday of Johnny Paycheck. Of course if you say that to your boss you can pretty much figure your paycheck will go right in the johnny.

Graffiti

Fish get chicken pox on a small scale.

JOKE: A grasshopper goes into a bar, and orders a beer. The bartender fills a mug and says, "You know, we have a drink here that's named after you."

The grasshopper takes a hit of the beer and says, "You mean to tell me you have a drink called Lester?"

June 1st

TODAY'S THOUGHT: "Election campaigns are like cleaning a window. The dirt is always on the other side." *—William H. Herles*

OBSERVANCE/EVENT: It's "National Repeat Day". It's "National Repeat Day".

Graffiti

Humpty Dumpty was pushed.

JOKE: Frick: I just can't lose weight no matter what.
Frack: Just stop thinking about desserts. Whatever you do, don't think of desserts.
Frick: Do you think I can?
Frack: Piece of cake.

June 2nd

TODAY'S THOUGHT: "Golf is like a love affair. If you don't take it seriously it's no fun; if you do take it seriously, it's apt to break your heart." *—Arnold Daly*

OBSERVANCE/EVENT: It's "Beaver Day"! Jerry Mathers was born on this day in 1948.

Graffiti

Confucius say: Ghost who gets lost in fog is mist.

JOKE: Heaven and Hell set up a baseball game and St. Peter gloated, "I don't know how you can win. We have Ruth, Drysdale, Mantle all up here."
"Maybe so," grinned the Devil, "but we got all the umpires down here."

June 3rd

TODAY'S THOUGHT: "Putting your best foot forward at least keeps it out of your mouth." —*Morris Mandel*

OBSERVANCE/EVENT: Funnyman Chuck Barris (TV producer of *The Dating Game, Newlywed Game* and *The Gong Show*) was born in Philadelphia on this date in 1929.

Graffiti
Flat feet are arch enemies.

JOKE: Did you hear the one about the guy who went to Las Vegas for some change and rest? The bellhops took the change and the casino took the rest.

June 4th

TODAY'S THOUGHT: "I always wondered why babies spend so much time sucking their thumbs. Then I tasted baby food." —*Robert Orben*

OBSERVANCE/EVENT: This day in 1937 saw the invention of the shopping cart. Since then cranky wheels have been driving everybody buggy.

Graffiti
Condense soup, not books!

JOKE: Husband: The doctor said, to relax, I should drink carrot juice following a hot bath.
Wife: Did it work?
Husband: I don't know. I haven't finished drinking the hot bath yet.

June 5th

TODAY'S THOUGHT: "I don't like spinach and I'm glad I don't, because if I liked it I'd eat it and I just hate it."
—*Clarence Darrow*

OBSERVANCE/EVENT: It's "National Bathroom Reading Week". People ask why can't Johnny read? "National Bathroom Reading Week" asks why can't they read in the johnny?

Graffiti
If you steal a clean slate, does it go on your record?

JOKE:

Q: Why did the Siamese twins move to London?

A: *So the other one could drive*

June 6th

TODAY'S THOUGHT: "Thanks to the Interstate Highway System, it is now possible to travel across the country from coast to coast without seeing anything."
—*Charles Kuralt*

OBSERVANCE/EVENT: It's "National Fragrance Week". This has nothing to do with "National Bathroom Reading Week". (See June 5.)

Graffiti
Save the whales. Collect the whole set.

JOKE: Patient: How do my x-rays look, Doc?
Doctor: Well, I just had a consultation and you're going to need surgery.
Patient: A consultation with another specialist?
Doctor: No, with my accountant.

June 7th

TODAY'S THOUGHT: "All my life, I always wanted to be somebody. Now I see that I should have been more specific." *—Jane Wagner*

OBSERVANCE/EVENT: It's officially "The Most Boring Day" of the year. What more can we say?

Graffiti

Termites never die. They live happily ever rafter.

JOKE: Woman: Doctor, my husband thinks he's a refrigerator.
Psychiatrist: That seems fairly harmless to me.
Woman: Yes, but he sleeps with his mouth open and the light keeps me awake.

June 8th

TODAY'S THOUGHT: "If you consider the contribution of plumbing to human life, the other sciences fade into insignificance." *—James Gorman*

OBSERVANCE/EVENT: Comedienne Joan Rivers was born in New York City on this date in 1937. She realized she was an unwanted child though, "When I saw that my bath toys were a toaster and a radio."

Graffiti

When in doubt, always grab the fullest glass.

JOKE:

Q: How can you tell when a lawyer is lying?

A: *His lips move*

June 9th

TODAY'S THOUGHT: "Have you heard the one about the husband who took a vacation in Hawaii and sent his wife a postcard? It said, 'The weather is here. Wish you were beautiful.'" —*Sanford Mims*

OBSERVANCE/EVENT: Bob Cummings debuted in Joplin, Missouri in 1910 while Jackie Mason was born Yacou Moshe Maza in 1934 in Sheboygan, Wisconsin and Michael J. Fox was a hit in Edmondton, Alberta on this day in 1961.

Graffiti

Dentures are little white lies.

JOKE: "Waiter! There's a fly in my soup!"
"That's funny. There were two of them when I left the kitchen."

June 10th

TODAY'S THOUGHT: "My father told me all about the birds and the bees. The liar. I went steady with a woodpecker till I was twenty-one." —*Bob Hope*

OBSERVANCE/EVENT: We admit to milking a lot of cheesy occasions in this book but this one is no bull. June is "National Dairy Month".

Graffiti

An astronomer is a night watchman.

JOKE:

Q: What do you call two thousand pounds of Chinese soup?

A: *Won ton*

June 11th

TODAY'S THOUGHT: "If a woman has to choose between catching a fly ball and saving an infant's life, she will choose to save the infant's life without even considering if there are men on base." —*Dave Barry*

OBSERVANCE/EVENT: On this date in 1939, comedic actor Gene Wilder made his first appearance in Milwaukee, Wisconsin.

Graffiti
I don't suffer from insanity. I enjoy every minute of it.

JOKE: Did you hear the one about the guy who would only play eighteen-hole golf courses because they matched his pants?

June 12th

TODAY'S THOUGHT: "When your friends begin to flatter you on how young you look, it's a sure sign you're getting old." —*Mark Twain*

OBSERVANCE/EVENT: Shazaam! Gomer Pyle added one more to the "Nabors-hood" as Jim Nabors was born on this date in 1932.

Graffiti
There's no future in time travel.

JOKE: He's so unlucky he once caught athlete's foot from the pool at Lourdes.

June 13th

TODAY'S THOUGHT: "Too bad that all the people who know how to run the country are busy driving taxicabs and cutting hair." —*George Burns*

OBSERVANCE/EVENT: It's "National Juggling Day". If you ever wanted to try your hand-eye coordination at juggling, tennis balls are good to start with. But if you have a hankering to begin by juggling bowling pins, a hard hat is definitely in order.

Graffiti
Death is life's way of telling you you've been fired.

JOKE: My friend got ill from inhaling second hand smoke. I warned him smoking with one hand was bad enough!

June 14th

TODAY'S THOUGHT: "If you want to know how old a woman is, ask her sister-in-law." —*Ed Howe*

OBSERVANCE/EVENT: "Flag Day" commemorates the day in 1777 when John Adams introduced a resolution to make the Stars 'n' Stripes our nation's official flag. Actually, Old Glory was his second choice but Abigail refused to donate a pair of her pantaloons for the cause.

Graffiti
Poets marry for better or verse.

JOKE: I had my cat neutered. He still hangs out all night with the other cats but now it's more in the role of consultant.

June 15th

TODAY'S THOUGHT: "Doorman: A man who stands out in front of hotels and acts as though he does not know how unimportant you are at home."
—*Anonymous*

OBSERVANCE/EVENT: Comedian/actor Jim Belushi was born in 1954 and Jim Varney started life in Ernest in 1949.

Graffiti
Draft beer, not people.

JOKE: Father: Son, do you realize that when Abraham Lincoln was your age he was already reading books studying to become an attorney?
Son: You're absolutely right, Dad, and by the time he was your age, he was already president.

June 16th

TODAY'S THOUGHT: "We should be grateful for subways. At least they've taken crime off the street."
—*Will Jordan*

OBSERVANCE/EVENT: Here's one you'll get a charge out of — it's "National Electricity Day" — but remember, that's no excuse to get lit.

Graffiti
The race to buy Father's Day gifts always ends in a tie!

JOKE: Husband: Why don't we go home early and make some whoopee? They say it's very good for the flu.
Wife: But I haven't got the flu.
Husband: So — you never heard of preventive medicine?

June 17th

TODAY'S THOUGHT: "Swearing was invented as a compromise between running away and fighting." —*Finley Peter Dunne*

OBSERVANCE/EVENT: Joe Piscopo felt the burn for the first time as the doctor slapped his gluteus maximus on this day in 1951. A few years later, he went back and slapped the doctor.

Graffiti
"Popcorn" is when fathers tell jokes.

JOKE: Did you hear the one about the farmer who planted cabbages and razor blades? He was hoping to raise cole slaw.

June 18th

TODAY'S THOUGHT: "I never got respect. I remember when I was a kid and played hide and seek...they wouldn't even look for me." —*Rodney Dangerfield*

OBSERVANCE/EVENT: Comic conductor Kay Kyser was born on this day in 1906 and, in 1952, comedienne Carol Kane was born.

Graffiti
Today is the yesterday you worried about tomorrow.

JOKE: "Hey, I heard a new one the other day. Did I tell it to you?"
"Was it funny?"
"Yeah."
"Then you haven't."

June 19th

TODAY'S THOUGHT: "I find television very educating. Every time somebody turns on the set, I go into another room and read a book." —*Groucho Marx*

OBSERVANCE/EVENT: Comic kitty Garfield puts another candle on his birthday lasagna today. He first went on the funny papers in 1978.

Graffiti

Better to understand a little than to misunderstand a lot.

JOKE: Did you hear the one about the basketball player who was so tall that when he fell down, he had to make two trips?

June 20th

TODAY'S THOUGHT: "The trouble with eating Italian food is that five or six days later you're hungry again." —*George Miller*

OBSERVANCE/EVENT: The day with the most daylight hours is fittingly also "Lighten Up America Day". You are urged to do something supremely silly. Maybe that nearby toilet paper roll would look good going off a balcony...

Graffiti

Support the Marcel Marceau Foundation because a mime is a terrible thing to waste.

JOKE: A guy died and left the world's shortest will. It read, "Being of sound mind, I spent my money."

June 21st

TODAY'S THOUGHT: "Comedy is the jazz of the English language." —*Rick Overton*

OBSERVANCE/EVENT: SCTV's Count Floyd, Joe Flaherty, was born on this day in 1940.

Graffiti
Change is inevitable, except from a vending machine.

JOKE: A sports car and a Mack truck get in a fender-bender on the I-10 in L.A.
The incensed sports car driver jumps up on the truck's running board, holds his hands out at an angle and screams, "Karate!"
The truck driver flattens him with a wallop to the head and yells, "Monkey wrench!"

June 22nd

TODAY'S THOUGHT: "Everything is funny as long as it's happening to somebody else." —*Will Rogers*

OBSERVANCE/EVENT: For police everywhere, this is a high hole-y day. The doughnut was invented in 1847.

Graffiti
You never realize how short a month is until you pay alimony.

JOKE:

Q: What do you get when you cross a crocodile with a sausage?

A: *A crockabaloney*

June 23rd

TODAY'S THOUGHT: "People who live in glass houses might as well answer the door." *—Morey Amsterdam*

OBSERVANCE/EVENT: It's "Cosmic Patience Day", a time to ponder how long we will have to wait for an answer to an interplanetary message sent in 1974 (probably about the same amount of time it takes your cable company to answer the phone).

Graffiti
Be different: Conform.

JOKE: I went to a paint store once and they had handicapped parking spaces for people who were color-blind.

June 24th

TODAY'S THOUGHT: "Just remember, when you're over the hill, you begin to pick up speed." *—Charles Schulz*

OBSERVANCE/EVENT: The modern era of "flying saucers" began in 1947 as Kenneth Arnold reported a formation of UFO's over Mt. Rainer, WA. Previously, the only reports of flying saucers came from nudists who spilled hot tea in their laps.

Graffiti
"Criminal Lawyer" is a redundancy.

JOKE:

Q: Where can you find a lawyer who doesn't lie, cheat or steal?

A: *In the cemetery*

June 25th

TODAY'S THOUGHT: "Remember when what is now called 'publicity' was called public shame and humiliation?" *—P.J. O'Rourke*

OBSERVANCE/EVENT: It's "Leon Day", a day just the opposite of Christmas. "Leon" is "Noel" spelled backwards and you're supposed to get, rather than give a gift.

Graffiti
No one cares how bad your English is as long as your Scotch is good.

JOKE: Two senior citizens are cuddling in bed on the morning of their 50th wedding anniversary.
He: Do you know what I'd do if I were 20 years younger?
She: Yes. You'd get up and go to work.

June 26th

TODAY'S THOUGHT: "Fun is like life insurance. The older you get the more it costs." *—Kin Hubbard*

OBSERVANCE/EVENT: It's "Clean Out Your Medicine Cabinet Day". *The Bathroom Joke Almanac* reminds you to safely dispose of those outdated medications: Uncle Charlie's Tooth Powder from 1957, Aunt Emma's secret ointment for "The Miseries" and that old can of Spray-On Hair you once mistook for deodorant.

Graffiti
Nothing political is correct.

JOKE: In downtown Philadelphia a tourist stops to ask a shop owner how far it is to the Liberty Bell.
"The way you're going, about 25,000 miles."

June 27th

TODAY'S THOUGHT: "There are too many comedians today. Soon the government will pay you not to do stand-up the same way they pay you not to grow wheat." —*Rita Rudner*

OBSERVANCE/EVENT: It's "National Fink Day" for rat finks, dirty finks and anybody named Fink.

Graffiti
To err is human, to moo bovine.

JOKE: Doctor: How did you get that terrible gash in your ear?
Man: I bit myself.
Doctor: It's anatomically impossible for man to bite himself on the ear.
Man: No, it's not. I was standing on a chair.

June 28th

TODAY'S THOUGHT: "Some lawyers are like laundries. They lose your shirt but still take you to the cleaners." —*Larry Wilde*

OBSERVANCE/EVENT: Comic/producer Mel Brooks was born Melvin Kaminsky on this day in 1928.

Graffiti
Everytime your ship comes in, the government unloads it.

JOKE: An absent-minded guy comes home from work. His wife says, "Where did you leave your umbrella?"
He says, "Gee, I don't know."
She says, "Well, when did you become aware that it was missing?"
He says, "Well, when it stopped raining, I reached up to close it and it was gone."

June 29th

TODAY'S THOUGHT: "About the time we think we can make ends meet, someone moves the ends."
—Herbert Hoover

OBSERVANCE/EVENT: A big day for armchair quarterbacks and couch potatoes everywhere...the television remote control made its TV debut in 1964.

Graffiti
A flashlight is only a case for holding dead batteries.

JOKE: A bore is someone who persists in holding his own views after we have enlightened him with ours.

June 30th

TODAY'S THOUGHT: "College is the best time of your life. Where else are your parents going to spend several thousand dollars a year just for you to go to a strange town and get drunk every night?" *—David Wood.*

OBSERVANCE/EVENT: David Alan Grier did his first improvisation on this date in 1955.

Graffiti
Those who indulge, bulge.

JOKE: A man walks into an Irish bar with an alligator on a leash. "Do you serve Americans here?" he asked.
"We sure do," replied the bartender.
"Great. Then I'll have a daiquiri and my 'gator will have an American."

July 1st

TODAY'S THOUGHT: "I don't want to be immortal through my work. I want to be immortal through not dying." *—Woody Allen*

OBSERVANCE/EVENT: On this date in 1952, Dan Akroyd was definitely not yet ready for prime time as he was born in Ottawa.

Graffiti

Warning: Dates on calendar are closer than they appear.

JOKE: Did you hear the one about the woman who made a fortune cleaning computers. Her slogan was "I do Windows."

July 2nd

TODAY'S THOUGHT: "There's a television commercial where a customer in a drug store has never heard of Preparation H. Where has he had his head?" *—Gallagher*

OBSERVANCE/EVENT: July is "Read an Almanac Month" to make people aware of what wonderful, entertaining, enriching, fabulous, absolutely indispensable things almanacs are. Modesty prevents us from saying any more.

Graffiti

Overweight is living beyond your seams.

JOKE: You know you're in a bad hotel when the number for room service is 911.

July 3rd

TODAY'S THOUGHT: "Smartness runs in my family. When I went to school I was so smart my teacher was in my class for five years." —*Gracie Allen*

OBSERVANCE/EVENT: The "Dog Days" of summer begin today. The ancients sacrificed a brown dog to appease the rage of Sirius, the Dog Star. Nowadays, we don't believe in such nonsense. We know summer swelter comes not from Sirius but from all those air conditioners blowing hot air out the window.

Graffiti

Money isn't everything — if it was, what would we buy with it?

JOKE: "The early bird catches the worm." It doesn't say much for the early worm, does it?

July 4th

TODAY'S THOUGHT: "It's a funny thing about our nation: July 4th is its birthday, but April 15th is when it collects the presents." —*Anonymous*

OBSERVANCE/EVENT: Not only was America born on this day but also one of its favorite funnymen, Neil Simon, began his first draft of life back in 1927.

Graffiti

The doctor may be a quack, but you still can't duck his bill.

JOKE: Two elephants are talking when one says to the other, "I don't care what they say, I can't remember a thing."

July 5th

TODAY'S THOUGHT: "Middle age is when a narrow waist and a broad mind begin to change places." —*Glenn Dorenbush*

OBSERVANCE/EVENT: Just when you thought the fireworks were over, comes this news: July is "National Baked Bean Month"!

Graffiti
It's not whether you win or lose, it's how you place the blame.

JOKE: Sid: My shop was burglarized last night and the thieves got everything.
Stan: That's terrible!
Sid: Not as bad as if they had broken in the night before. I just finished marking everything down 50%!

July 6th

TODAY'S THOUGHT: "Procrastination is the art of keeping up with yesterday." —*Don Marquis*

OBSERVANCE/EVENT: The weekend following July fourth is "National Nude Weekend". It's also "National Stay Away From Wicker Furniture Days".

Graffiti
Roosters crow; hens deliver.

JOKE: And then there was the fighter whose boxing career didn't go so well although he was able to sell advertising space on the soles of his shoes.

July 7th

TODAY'S THOUGHT: "If the Lord had wanted people to fly, He would have made it simpler for people to get to the airport." —*Milton Berle*

OBSERVANCE/EVENT: The first full week of July is "National Canned Luncheon Meat Week". Yum-Yum, there's some Spam good eatin' up in Austin, Minnesota, the Canned Meat Capital Of The World.

Graffiti
Kangaroos drink hopscotch.

JOKE:

Q: What does a mobster buried in cement eventually become?

A: *A hardened criminal*

July 8th

TODAY'S THOUGHT: "I talk to myself because I like dealing with a better class of people." —*Jackie Mason*

OBSERVANCE/EVENT: The Declaration of Independence was read publicly for the first time on this date in 1776 in Philadelphia. By the way, you know where it was signed, don't you? At the bottom.

Graffiti
Henry Ford's diary is an autobiography.

JOKE: Patient: Doc, I have some dimes stuck in my ear.
Doctor: How long have they been there?
Patient: About six months.
Doctor: Why didn't you come in sooner?
Patient: I didn't need the money.

July 9th

TODAY'S THOUGHT: "Sometimes I think the surest sign that intelligent life exists elsewhere in the univers is that none of it has tried to contact us." *—Bill Watterson*

OBSERVANCE/EVENT: On this day in 1872, John Blondel invented the world's first donut cutter. Law enforcement officers everywhere plan to give him a 21-dunk salute.

Graffiti
Dolphins have a porpoise in life.

JOKE:

Q: Why was the man who thought he was a dog afraid to go to the psychiatrist?

A: *He was afraid he wouldn't be allowed on the couch.*

July 10th

TODAY'S THOUGHT: "I'm desperately trying to figure out why kamikaze pilots wore helmets." *—Dave Edison*

OBSERVANCE/EVENT: It's "Lady Godiva Day", commemorating her famous horseback ride through Coventry while totally naked, circa 1040. (This event gave new meaning to the term "riding bareback".)

Graffiti
"G" is the end of everything.

JOKE: A woman walking down Fifth Avenue is accosted by an animal rights protestor.
"How dare you wear that fur coat? Do you know how much the poor animal suffered just so you could wear that thing?"
"Oh," replied the woman, "so you know my husband?"

July 11th

TODAY'S THOUGHT: "Only one man in a thousand is a leader of men — the other 999 follow women." —*Groucho Marx*

OBSERVANCE/EVENT: The United States Marines began their long march from the halls of Montezuma to the shores of Tripoli on this date back in 1798. Of course, after that Montezuma run-in, their motto was "We're Looking For A Few Good Men's Rooms".

Graffiti
Ghosts live on dead ends.

JOKE: Waiter: I'll have you know that we run a very clean restaurant here.
Waitee: You must — everything tastes like soap!

July 12th

TODAY'S THOUGHT: "Parents often talk about the younger generation as if they didn't have anything to do with it." —*Funny, Funny World*

OBSERVANCE/EVENT: Two of the all-time greats of comedy first stepped up on the world's stage today: Milton Berle in 1908 and Bill Cosby in 1937.

Graffiti
A fortuneteller has medium prices.

JOKE: Hospital scene—
Distraught mother: Doctor, doctor. My son's been run over by a steamroller! Where is he?
Doctor: Ah, yes... the steamroller victim. He's in rooms 210, 211 and 212.

July 13th

TODAY'S THOUGHT: "The formula for water is H_2O. Is the formula for an ice cube H_2O squared?" *—Lily Tomlin*

OBSERVANCE/EVENT: The Cheech half of Cheech and Chong, Cheech Marin, was born in 1946.

Graffiti

How long a minute is depends on which side of the bathroom door you're on.

JOKE: Woman: Help! My house is on fire! Come quick!
Dispatcher: OK, calm down. Now how do we get there?
Woman: Whatsamatter? Don't you have that big red truck anymore?

July 14th

TODAY'S THOUGHT: "To my wife double parking means on top of another car." *—Dave Barry*

OBSERVANCE/EVENT: The prince of pratfalls, ex-President Gerald R. Ford, was born today in 1913.

Graffiti

A chimney sweeper's job soots him.

JOKE: One Martian comes up to another Martian standing next to a mailbox and a fire alarm box.
"Say, who are your two friends?" says the second Martian winking.
"Oh, forget them," replies the first Martian. "The fat one with the big mouth just stands there and if you touch the redhead, she starts shrieking."

July 15th

TODAY'S THOUGHT: "I'm not the best dresser. Every year Goodwill gives me $500 not to clean out my closets." —*Pat Cooper*

OBSERVANCE/EVENT: Ever wonder when "St. Swithun's Day" is? Well, wonder no more. The former bishop of Winchester was buried in a downpour on this day, and legend has it that if it rains today, it will rain for the next 40 days.

Graffiti

Sir Lancelot's horse was a knight mare.

JOKE: Did you hear the one about the guy who joined a group of cloistered monks? He had to leave because of his paranoia. He kept feeling everybody wasn't talking about him.

July 16th

TODAY'S THOUGHT: "You might be a redneck if your TV gets 512 channels but you go outside to use the bathroom." —*Jeff Foxworthy*

OBSERVANCE/EVENT: A dark day to park...the first parking meters were installed in 1935 in Oklahoma City.

Graffiti

Behind every successful man is an IRS agent!

JOKE: Slacker #1: If your wife made you go out and look for a job what would you look for?
Slacker #2: A new wife

July 17th

TODAY'S THOUGHT: "Our language is funny — a fat chance and slim chance are the same thing." *—J. Gustav White*

OBSERVANCE/EVENT: Phyllis Diller came into the world on this day in 1917 and like she says, she was so ugly the doctor spanked her mother.

Graffiti

If you wanted control, you should have married your remote!

JOKE: Then there was the company president who was in the hospital recovering from surgery. He received a get-well card from the board of directors who wrote, "We wish you a speedy recovery... by a vote of four to three."

July 18th

TODAY'S THOUGHT: "The average dog is a nicer person than the average person." *—Andy Rooney*

OBSERVANCE/EVENT: Red Skelton and his alter egos, Freddie the Freeloader and Clem Kadiddlehopper, were born on this day in 1913.

Graffiti

Money isn't everything but it keeps you in touch with the kids.

JOKE: Fred and Ethel were having a discussion about family finances. Finally the wife lost her temper. "If it weren't for my money, this house wouldn't be here!" The husband replied, "Listen, Ethel, if it weren't for your money I wouldn't be here!"

July 19th

TODAY'S THOUGHT: "It's hard to feel morally superior to someone who gets up earlier than you do." *—Mary Gordon*

OBSERVANCE/EVENT: It's "Bloomer Day" marking the day in 1848 when Amelia Bloomer introduced the garment that was to bear her name.

Graffiti
Fortunetellers have a ball.

JOKE: Personnel Interviewer: Are you a yes man?
Job Applicant: Maybe.

July 20th

TODAY'S THOUGHT: "My teacher told me that today was the first day of the rest of my life. That explains why I didn't do yesterday's homework." *—Lorne Elliot*

OBSERVANCE/EVENT: It's "Creative Ice Cream Flavor Day". Put Baskin Robbins to shame. Let your imagination run wild. How about Zinc Oxide Mocha SPF #15? Or maybe Banana Nut Oat Bran or a nice Spinach-Bubble gum sundae?

Graffiti
Dieters are people who are thick and tired of it.

JOKE: He: I accidentally swallowed my watch.
She: Does it hurt?
He: Only when I try to wind it.

July 21st

TODAY'S THOUGHT: "Baseball is a sport in which men who have rested all winter need weeks of spring training for a summer of playing games."
—Doug Larsen

OBSERVANCE/EVENT: Comedic actor Don Knotts was born in 1924; Robin Williams opened in 1952; and Jon Lovitz came into the world in 1957...no lie.

Graffiti
Confucius say: If people string you along, you become real yo-yo.

JOKE: A drunk goes up to an elevator and hits the 'down' button. The doors open, he steps in but there's no elevator. He plummets twelve stories to the bottom of the shaft. He gets up, brushes himself off and says, "Maybe I should have pushed 'up'."

July 22nd

TODAY'S THOUGHT: "No wonder golf is a sport in which tempers grow very thin; it's the only game in which players are teed off when they begin."
—George O. Ludcke

OBSERVANCE/EVENT: Humorist and game show fixture Orson Bean first joined the panel of *What's My Line?* in 1928.

Graffiti
Environmental activists are ecomaniacs!

JOKE: He was the world's cheapest counterfeiter. He was so tight, he still had the first dollar he ever printed.

July 23rd

TODAY'S THOUGHT: "There are three stages in an actor's career: 'Who is he?'; 'There he is!' and 'My God! Is he *still* around?'" —*Jack Oakie*

OBSERVANCE/EVENT: The first U.S. swimming school opened in Boston in 1827. Their marking system was "pass/flail".

Graffiti
Honk If You Like Noise Pollution.

JOKE: Frick: I called my psychiatrist and told him that I thought I had kleptomania.
Frack: What did he do?
Frick: He told me to take something for it.

July 24th

TODAY'S THOUGHT: "The phrase 'The Melting Pot' used to mean the United States of America. Now it means you put the wrong container in the microwave."—*Robert Orben*

OBSERVANCE/EVENT: Instant coffee was invented on this day in 1938. Unfortunately, it would be many years yet before they cracked the formula for hot water.

Graffiti
Middle Age: When your hairline's going up and your gumline's going down.

JOKE: His resume says he was on the inside track at Smucker's. We looked it up. Turns out he was always in a jam.

July 25th

TODAY'S THOUGHT: "Old men are fond of giving advice to console themselves for being no longer in a position to give bad examples."
—Francois de La Rochefoucauld

OBSERVANCE/EVENT: The lowest natural temperature ever recorded was set in Antarctica in 1983. The thermometer reached 129 degrees below zero. (It was so cold politicians had their hands in their own pockets!)

Graffiti
A chef is a man for all seasonings.

JOKE: A man told his doctor that he suspected he had a split personality so the doctor charged him double!

July 26th

TODAY'S THOUGHT: "When I was born I was so surprised I couldn't talk for a year and a half."
—Gracie Allen

OBSERVANCE/EVENT: Gracie Allen was born this day in 1906; Vivian Vance debuted in 1912; and humorist Jean Shepherd started gathering material for his autobiographical stories in 1929.

Graffiti
By the time you're old enough to be nostalgic, your memory's too short.

JOKE: His references included a letter from a state official who said, "We're sorry we let him get away." It turned out to be from the warden.

July 27th

TODAY'S THOUGHT: "The second day of a diet is always easier than the first. By the second day you're off it." —*Jackie Gleason*

OBSERVANCE/EVENT: The youngest tyke of the Van Dykes, banjo-pickin' Jerry, was born on this day in 1931.

> **Graffiti**
> *The leading cause of death in lab mice is research.*

JOKE: Teacher: Welcome to your first day of school. The class rules are no talking, no gum chewing and if you have to go the bathroom, just hold up one finger.
Weisenheimer: How's that going to help?

July 28th

TODAY'S THOUGHT: "Nothing in fine print is ever good news." —*Andy Rooney.*

OBSERVANCE/EVENT: One of Hollywood's most famous comedy scriptwriters/producers, Norman Lear, (*All in the Family, Maude*) was born on this date in 1922.

> **Graffiti**
> *Earthquake predictors are faultfinders.*

JOKE: At the side of the road:
Driver: What seems to be the trouble, officer?
Cop: Bad news, sir. Your wife fell out of the car ten miles back.
Driver: Oh, thank goodness. I thought I was going deaf!

July 29th

TODAY'S THOUGHT: "Why does the Air Force need expensive new bombers? Have the people we've been bombing over the years been complaining?"
—George Wallace

OBSERVANCE/EVENT: It's "Rain Day" in Waynesburg, Pennsylvania where legend has it that rain will fall on July 29 as it has for most years. In honor of the occasion, we bring you this groaner: What's worse than raining cats and dogs? Hailing taxis.

Graffiti
Genetic engineering is heir styling.

JOKE: Eve: Do you love me, Adam?
Adam: Who else?

July 30th

TODAY'S THOUGHT: "Kissing is a custom in France. We kiss a man we haven't seen in five years — or a woman we haven't seen in five minutes."
—Maurice Chevalier

OBSERVANCE/EVENT: Sitcom actress Delta Burke (Suzanne Sugarbaker on *Designing Women*) was born on this date in 1956.

Graffiti
Why are there so many more horse's rear ends than horses?

JOKE: Doctor: Now take this medication only with meals. That'll be $100.
Patient: But Doc, I'm broke. I haven't eaten in a week.
Doctor: Great — then the pills will last a lot longer.

July 31st

TODAY'S THOUGHT: "I wouldn't mind being the last man on earth... just to see if all those girls were telling me the truth." *—Ronnie Shakes*

OBSERVANCE/EVENT: Henry Perky patented Shredded Wheat on this day in 1893. It was an accidental discovery. Actually, he was trying to perfect the world's smallest hay-baler.

Graffiti

For sale: Ex-wife. Take over payments.

JOKE: Job applicant: Yes, I'm a good lumberjack. Ever heard of the Sahara Forest?
Foreman: You mean the Sahara Desert.
Job applicant: Sure, that's what they call it now.

August 1st

TODAY'S THOUGHT: "August is the month that the collapsible wading pool you bought in June finally does." —*Changing Times*

OBSERVANCE/EVENT: Dom DeLuise was no doubt the bounciest baby boy around on this day in 1933.

Graffiti
Possessiveness is a state of mine.

JOKE: Frick: I rented a summer place in the Hamptons. It's right on the beach.
Frack: Is it a big house?
Frick: Big? Four stories...five when the tide goes out.

August 2nd

TODAY'S THOUGHT: "If I could drop dead right now, I'd be the happiest man alive!" —*Pete Townshend*

OBSERVANCE/EVENT: In 1892 Charles Wheeler patented the first escalator. A jokebook publisher friend of his was the first person to ride the escalator. Unfortunately, there was a power outage and the poor guy was trapped for hours.

Graffiti
If at first you don't succeed,
that pretty much does it for skydiving.

JOKE: Two goats are eating at the town dump. One goat finds a roll of film and starts munching on it. The other goat says, "How's the film?"
The first goat responds, "I liked the book better."

August 3rd

TODAY'S THOUGHT: "At 82, I feel like a 20 year-old but, unfortunately, there's never one around."
—Milton Berle

OBSERVANCE/EVENT: Director John Landis, of *Animal House* fame, was born in 1950.

Graffiti

General Custer was the first to wear an arrow shirt.

JOKE: Frick: Did you hear about the blaze in the showgirls' dressing room?
Frack: Was it bad?
Frick: Bad? It took three hours to put the fire out and three days to put the firemen out.

August 4th

TODAY'S THOUGHT: "Assume nothing. Inside every dumb blond there may be a very smart brunette."
—Ann Landers

OBSERVANCE/EVENT: It's okay to get excited but don't pop your cork. Champagne was invented on this day in 1693.

Graffiti

Get a high school education...enroll in the college of your choice.

JOKE: Did you hear the one about the movie theater owner who passed away? Services were held at 2:40, 4:30, 6:30 and 9:45.

August 5th

TODAY'S THOUGHT: "Ever read the label on a deodorant can? 'Caution, content highly inflammable. May explode.' I don't want nothin' under my arm that's gonna explode!" —*Richard Pryor*

OBSERVANCE/EVENT: Little Orphan Annie was born in 1924. Imagine that! Little Orphan Annie is old enough to be on Medicare — and get that pupil transplant she's always dreamed of.

Graffiti
A bird in the hand is better than one over your head.

JOKE: Then there was the tattoo artist who was fired for having designs on her clients.

August 6th

TODAY'S THOUGHT: "A salesman is a fellow with a smile on his face, a shine on his shoes and a lousy territory." —*George Gobel*

OBSERVANCE/EVENT: Today in 1911 "Waaahhhh!" was first heard from Lucille Ball.

Graffiti
Smoking cures weight problems...eventually.

JOKE: Frick: How's your son doing nowadays?
Frack: He's with the FBI.
Frick: Really?
Frack: Yeah. They picked him up in Chicago.

August 7th

TODAY'S THOUGHT: "Television is a device that permits people who haven't anything to do to watch people who can't do anything." —*Fred Allen*

OBSERVANCE/EVENT: It's "Sneak Zucchini Onto Your Neighbor's Porch Night" — the only way to get rid of that bumper crop of zucchini that's taking over your yard. Be careful not to trespass, however, or your neighbor might press charges and you'll end up in a squash court.

Graffiti

Great minds run in the same gutter.

JOKE: And then there was the guy who claimed he made excellent grades at Harvard. It turned out he drove a bulldozer building the parking lot.

August 8th

TODAY'S THOUGHT: "If God had wanted us to plant gardens, he wouldn't have created supermarkets." —*James Dent*

OBSERVANCE/EVENT: Betty Boop debuted this day in 1930 in the Max Fleischer cartoon *Dizzy Dishes*.

Graffiti

Here I sit, my dignity tarnished.
The toilet seat was freshly varnished.

JOKE: "Well, I got good news and bad news at the doctor's today."
"What's the good news?"
"He found out what I had."
"And what's the bad news?"
"He took every penny of it."

August 9th

TODAY'S THOUGHT: "It took a genius to develop an aspirin bottle that couldn't be opened by a child capable of operating a VCR." —*Doug Larsen*

OBSERVANCE/EVENT: The first full week of August is "National Smile Week" and on this day in 1944, Smokey the Bear was born. All of which means that today, you should grin and bear it.

Graffiti
Confucious say: Man who fall in vat of molten glass make spectacle of self.

JOKE: The answer is: Intense
And the question? Where do campers sleep?

August 10th

TODAY'S THOUGHT: "An ounce of pretension is worth a pound of manure." —*Steve E. Clark*

OBSERVANCE/EVENT: August is "National Psychic Month", but then, you already knew that, didn't you?

Graffiti
Prune juice makes the going great.

JOKE: A guy visits a nudist colony. He sees a man with a beard down to his knees walking by. The visitor asks, "Who's that?"
"That's Fuzzy! Someone has to go out for the bagels and coffee."

August 11th

TODAY'S THOUGHT: "There are two types of people in this world, good and bad. The good sleep better, but the bad seem to enjoy the waking hours much more." —*Woody Allen*

OBSERVANCE/EVENT: It's "Presidential Joke Day", the anniversary of President Reagan's 1984 remarks about bombing Russia that were inadvertently picked up by live mikes. Feel free to relieve any frustration you may have regarding the Chief Executive — after all, the rest of the year the joke's on you!

Graffiti

Figures don't lie but girdles redistribute the truth.

JOKE: Did you hear about the girl who's so skinny she has to run around in the shower just to get wet?

August 12th

TODAY'S THOUGHT: "I have to exercise in the morning before my brain figures out what I'm doing." —*Marsha Doble*

OBSERVANCE/EVENT: Scorch that skin and heat your hide — It's "Get A Tan Day", celebrated annually on the birthday of George Hamilton.

Graffiti

A sleeping bag is a nap sack.

JOKE: Knock, knock.
Who's there?
Effervescent...
Effervescent who?
Effervescent for wine, women and song, I'd be a pretty good husband.

August 13th

TODAY'S THOUGHT: "Friends may come and go, but enemies accumulate." —*Thomas Jones*

OBSERVANCE/EVENT: It's "International Left-handers Day" and remember this adage: If the right side of the mind controls the left side of the body, this means only left-handed people are in their right minds.

Graffiti

To err is human —
to blame it on somebody else is even more human.

JOKE: Then there was the guy who was so bald that instead of a toupee he had to wear a three-pee.

August 14th

TODAY'S THOUGHT: "The way money goes so fast these days they should paint racing stripes on it." —*Mark Russell*

OBSERVANCE/EVENT: The wild and crazy Steve Martin ended his nine-month engagement at his first venue, The Mother's Womb in Waco, Texas on this day in 1945.

Graffiti

Be true to your teeth and they won't be false to you.

JOKE:

Q: What's the difference between one yard and two yards?

A: *Usually, a fence*

August 15th

TODAY'S THOUGHT: "August is when you look at your utility bill and lose your cool." *—Phillip Lazarus*

OBSERVANCE/EVENT: It's "National Relaxation Day". We'd tell you more about it, but hey, we're observing it, too.

Graffiti
Give a dandelion an inch and it takes over a yard.

JOKE: Son: Well, Dad, I finally got my merit badge.
Father: That's great, Son. What was it for?
Son: For fixing bicycle horns.
Father: They give merit badges for fixing bicycle horns?
Son: Sure. In fact, the Boy Scouts' motto is "Beep Repaired".

August 16th

TODAY'S THOUGHT: "If you believe there is a solution, you're part of the problem." *—George Carlin*

OBSERVANCE/EVENT: It's "Joe Miller's Joke Day", commemorating the 18th century English actor who inspired the very first jokebook (which is not only an historical and precedent-setting publication, it's also in the public domain so we can steal the author blind!).

Graffiti
William Tell wore contact lenses.

JOKE: "Heard you got hit by lightning on the golf course."
"Yep."
"Did you learn anything from the experience?"
"Yeah. If God wants to play through, let Him."

August 17th

TODAY'S THOUGHT: "Few people think more than two or three times a year. I have made an international reputation for myself thinking once or twice a week." *—George Bernard Shaw*

OBSERVANCE/EVENT: On the Saturday nearest Woodstock Weekend, the 15th to 17th, all ex-Flower Children celebrate "Hippie Day". It's a happening, man — far out, dig it — get out your old groovy jeans and hope your old groovy still fits into them. Peace.

Graffiti
The only friend you can buy for money is a dog.

JOKE: And then there was the cannibal who had his friends for dinner.

August 18th

TODAY'S THOUGHT: "A hair in the head is worth two in the brush." *—Oliver Herford*

OBSERVANCE/EVENT: It's "Bad Poetry Day" so dabble in some iambic pentameter or whip up some haiku.

Graffiti
Cookbooks are full of stirring passages.

JOKE: A guy comes running from the woods of Montana, yelling, "I just shot an elk!"
One of the locals says to him, "Are you sure? I never saw any elk here."
"Absolutely. There's a membership card in his wallet."

August 19th

TODAY'S THOUGHT: "The truly great things happen when a genius is alone. This is true especially among golfers." *—J.R. Coulson*

OBSERVANCE/EVENT: It's "National Aviation Day" and "Go To The Track Day" so combine the events — take off and go to the track.

Graffiti

Humpty Dumpty is just a shell of his former self.

JOKE: Frack: Great vacation. We stayed at a five star hotel; a beautiful, spacious suite, fantastic view, all the amenities.
Frick: Really?
Frack: Yeah. And the towels there were so thick, we could hardly get our suitcase closed!

August 20th

TODAY'S THOUGHT: "Why is it when you're seven today is forever and tomorrow never; but when you're 70, tomorrow's yesterday before you knew it was today?" *—Sue Jane Purcell*

OBSERVANCE/EVENT: If your 'do doesn't, if your style is vile or your cut is in a rut, don't despair — it's "Bad Hair Day" observed every year on the birthday of Don King. Just turn your head and coiff.

Graffiti

Make your dreams come true...wake up!

JOKE: Dudley is applying for a job as an assistant's assistant. The office manager looks over his application and says, "You've been fired from every job you've had!"

Dudley says, "Yessir. I'm no quitter."

August 21st

TODAY'S THOUGHT: "My wife was in labor for thirty-two hours and I was faithful to her the whole time." *—Jonathan Katz*

OBSERVANCE/EVENT: The summer is two-thirds over. Have you taken any time to goof off yet. It's "Sit Back And Relax Day", a special occasion to while away a summer day. (Note: Keep this book handy in case your wife questions the validity of the holiday.)

Graffiti
Dentists are always looking down in the mouth.

JOKE:

Q: If two wrongs don't make a right, what do two rights make?

A: *An airplane*

August 22nd

TODAY'S THOUGHT: "Talk is cheap... except when Congress does it." *—Colleen Hightower*

OBSERVANCE/EVENT: TV comediennes Valerie Harper and Cindy Williams share the birthday if not the year. Valerie was born in 1940 and Cindy came along in 1947.

Graffiti
Look out for lawyers who say they're on your side... so is appendicitis.

JOKE: There's a new drink out called the Gin Dandy, made of equal parts milk, sugar and gin. The milk gives you energy, the sugar gives you pep and the gin gives you ideas of what to do with all that pep and energy.

August 23rd

TODAY'S THOUGHT: "I can't take a well-tanned person seriously." —*Cleveland Amory*

OBSERVANCE/EVENT: Three "Cheers" for comedic actress Shelley Long who was born on this date in 1949 in Fort Wayne, Indiana.

Graffiti
Failure follows the line of least persistence!

JOKE: Fred: How is it that your company gets such great salespeople?
Red: We send our trainees out to rent an apartment and, if they succeed, we give them their own territory.
Fred: So how do they prove themselves?
Red: When they knock on the landlord's door, they're carrying a tuba.

August 24th

TODAY'S THOUGHT: "Ever notice that people who are wrong seem to talk louder than anyone else?" —*Andy Rooney*

OBSERVANCE/EVENT: It's "Waffle Iron Day" commemorating the invention of the waffle iron in 1869. Prior to that, everyone's waffles were horribly wrinkled.

Graffiti
Be obscure clearly.

JOKE:
Q: Why can't you drive a golf ball?
A: *It doesn't have a steering wheel.*

August 25th

TODAY'S THOUGHT: "I now believe in reincarnation. Tonight's monologue is going to come back as a dog." *—Johnny Carson*

OBSERVANCE/EVENT: It's "007 Day", celebrated on the birthday of Sean Connery. Have a glass of iced tea in celebration — shaken, not stirred.

Graffiti
Be kind to railroad engineers...
their work gives them a tender behind.

JOKE: Customer: Tell me, waiter, do you have any wild rice?
Waiter: No, sir, but we could take some tame rice and irritate it.

August 26th

TODAY'S THOUGHT: "We usually meet all our relatives only at funerals where someone always observes, 'Too bad we can't get together more often.'" *—Sam Levenson*

OBSERVANCE/EVENT: Forget gun powder, pasta and astronomy. The greatest discovery ever to come out of China was introduced on this day in 580 — toilet paper.

Graffiti
Confidence is that feeling you have before you know better.

JOKE: Ever notice that the toast of the town is usually the person with the most bread?

August 27th

TODAY'S THOUGHT: "Behind every successful man you'll find a woman who has nothing to wear." *—James Stewart*

OBSERVANCE/EVENT: It's the anniversary of the drilling of the first oil well in 1859 — the first successful oil well anyway. And you know what they say: oil's well that ends well.

> **Graffiti**
> *Being a rabbit farmer is a hare-raising experience.*

JOKE:

Q: Who is Noah's wife?

A: *Joan of Arc*

August 28th

TODAY'S THOUGHT: "To err is human; to admit it, superhuman." *—Doug Larsen*

OBSERVANCE/EVENT: United Parcel Service was founded in 1907. It would have been founded sooner but the Post Office lost its license application in the mail.

> **Graffiti**
> *Any time you don't want anything, you get it.*

JOKE: A 75 year-old tycoon tells his friend he's just gotten engaged to a gorgeous 21 year-old blonde. His friend says, "I know you've got a lot of money but, still in all, how could you attract a girl that young and that beautiful?"

"I told her I was 95."

August 29th

TODAY'S THOUGHT: "If people don't want to come to the ballpark, how are you gonna stop them?" —*Yogi Berra*

OBSERVANCE/EVENT: It's "National Plastic Surgery Day", observed annually on Michael Jackson's birthday...or should we say the birthday of his first nose?

Graffiti
Lord give me patience...and hurry!

JOKE: A guy comes home and finds his wife, a noted psychic, standing at the door with a rolling pin. "You no good louse," she growled, "and just where were you until 3 A.M. tomorrow morning?"

August 30th

TODAY'S THOUGHT: "One day my father took me aside and left me there." —*Jackie Vernon*

OBSERVANCE/EVENT: "The Absent Minded Professor", Fred MacMurray, was born on this date in 1908 in Kankakee, Illinois.

Graffiti
The young and the old know all the answers.
In between, we don't even know the questions.

JOKE: Doctor: Henry, you've been my patient for fifty years and I have to tell you that what you're considering is dangerous. I mean a 93 year-old man marrying a 19 year-old girl. That could prove fatal.
Henry: Hey Doc, the way I look at it, if she dies, she dies!

August 31st

TODAY'S THOUGHT: "Did you hear the one about the lawyer who frequented only posh restaurants? He was an ambiance chaser." *—Emo Phillips*

OBSERVANCE/EVENT: Comedian and actor Buddy Hackett was born in Brooklyn on this day back in 1924.

Graffiti

The universe is expanding...why shouldn't you?

JOKE: "Crumstead, I happen to know that yesterday, when you took off from work when you were supposedly sick, you played golf at the Greenwood Country Club."

"That's not true, sir," Crumstead protested, "and I have the fish to prove it!"

September 1st

TODAY'S THOUGHT: "The only thing that holds a marriage together is the husband bein' big enough to step back and see where his wife is wrong." —*Archie Bunker*

OBSERVANCE/EVENT: Ernestine the operator, Edith Anne and all of Lily Tomlin's other characters were born on this day in 1939.

Graffiti
Sopranos are trebel-shooters.

JOKE: Frick: I think this milk I bought is outdated.
Frack: How can you tell?
Frick: Because the missing person on the carton is Jimmy Hoffa.

September 2nd

TODAY'S THOUGHT: "Never try to impress a woman, because if you do she'll expect you to keep up to the standard for the rest of your life." —*W.C. Fields*

OBSERVANCE/EVENT: September is "Be Kind To Editors and Writers" month so if you notice any errers in this book, it wood be much appreciated if you forgive them,

Graffiti
Voodoo schools teach hex education.

JOKE: A guy sees a lion approaching, falls to his knees, and prays to the Lord in hopes of being saved. All of a sudden, the lion kneels too. The guy says, "You're saying prayers, too?"
"No. Grace."

September 3rd

TODAY'S THOUGHT: "Any guy who has hair on his head is overdressed." —*Joe Garagiola*

OBSERVANCE/EVENT: In 1639, the first lawyer was disbarred in America. One down, two million to go.

Graffiti
A penny saved is a penny taxed!

JOKE:

Q: How many doctors does it take to change a light bulb?

A: *That depends on how much life insurance the light bulb has.*

September 4th

TODAY'S THOUGHT: "I bought an ant farm. I don't know where I'm gonna find a tractor that small." —*Steven Wright*

OBSERVANCE/EVENT: A twitch of the nose to Dick York (aka Darrin Stephens, the husband of Samantha in TV's *Bewitched*) who was born on this date in 1928.

Graffiti
Gossips have a great sense of rumor.

JOKE: Did you hear about the Pekingese dog that married a tomcat? Now they have a Peking Tom.

September 5th

TODAY'S THOUGHT: "People who sleep like a baby usually don't have one." —*Leo J. Burke*

OBSERVANCE/EVENT: The world first said "Hi Bob!" to Bob Newhart, born in Chicago in 1929. Also, in honor of Bob's most famous character, it's "National Shrink Day".

Graffiti
My elected representatives went to Washington and all I lost was my shirt!

JOKE:

Q: Where do you find a turtle without feet?

A: *Exactly where you left him*

September 6th

TODAY'S THOUGHT: "My mom was a little weird. When I was little my mom would make chocolate frosting and she let me lick the beaters. And then she'd turn them off." —*Marty Cohen*

OBSERVANCE/EVENT: Alumni of two great TV comedies share this birthdate: *Laugh-In*'s Jo Anne Worley, 1937 and *SNL*'s Jane Curtin, 1947.

Graffiti
Save string...have a ball.

JOKE: An egotistical earthworm is crawling along the ground when, alongside him, he sees the most beautiful earthworm ever. "Hey, Babe," the earthworm says, "where have you been all my life?"
"Get a life, buster. I'm your other end."

September 7th

TODAY'S THOUGHT: "Kids are like husbands. They're fine as long as they're someone else's."
—*Marsha Warfield*

OBSERVANCE/EVENT: The American Association for Nude Recreation got its start in 1931 and the Miss America Pageant first gave Atlantic City a post-Labor Day boost in 1921. Bet you're thinking why don't they just combine the two events?

Graffiti
A friend in need is a friend to avoid.

JOKE: Diner: Waiter, there's a fly in my soup!
Waiter: Don't worry, sir, he's used to the heat.

September 8th

TODAY'S THOUGHT: "I have just learned that penguins are monogamous for life, which doesn't really surprise me all that much because they all look exactly alike. It's not like they're going to meet a better-looking penguin someday." —*Ellen DeGeneres*

OBSERVANCE/EVENT: That Caesar who ruled in the days when Comedy was King, Sid, was born this day in 1922. Also born today: Peter Sellers, 1925 and the comic strip *Blondie*, in 1930.

Graffiti
I fixed Olivia Newton's John.

JOKE:

Q: How many lawyer jokes are there?

A: *None. They're all true.*

September 9th

TODAY'S THOUGHT: "It took me seventeen years to get three thousand hits in baseball. I did it in one afternoon on the golf course." —*Hank Aaron*

OBSERVANCE/EVENT: Sitcom actress Kristy McNichol (*Family, Empty Nest*) was born on this date in Los Angeles in 1962.

Graffiti
Dating is a Hit-on-Miss proposition.

JOKE: A new bank employee was counting money very fast. The president was impressed and asked, "Where did you learn your math?"
The employee replied, "Yale."
"That's terrific. By the way, what's your name?"
"Yohnson."

September 10th

TODAY'S THOUGHT: "We hope that when the insects take over the world, they will remember with gratitude how we took them along on all our picnics."
—*Bill Vaughn*

OBSERVANCE/EVENT: It's "International Make-Up Day", a day to remember someone who wronged you and bury the hatchet...hopefully in the ground!

Graffiti
A fool and his money are soon elected.

JOKE: Doctor: Well Mr. Jones, I've completed your physical and I'd say you'll live to be ninety.
Mr. Jones: I ***am*** ninety!
Doctor: See, what'd I tell you?

September 11th

TODAY'S THOUGHT: "When those waiters ask me if I want some fresh ground pepper, I ask if they have any aged pepper." —*Andy Rooney*

OBSERVANCE/EVENT: On "No News Is Good News Day" everyone is urged to duck all newscasts, weather reports or sports scores today and remain blissfully ignorant of the turmoil all around us. One exception — you may want to check the lottery number!

Graffiti
It's a small world, but I wouldn't want to paint it.

JOKE: Did you hear the one about the egotistical sports star who had help writing his autobiography? He used a boast writer.

September 12th

TODAY'S THOUGHT: "The Concorde was great. It travels at twice the speed of sound which is fun except you can't hear the movie until two hours after you land." —*Howie Mandel*

OBSERVANCE/EVENT: America caught its first *Taxi*, as the classic series premiered on this date in 1978.

Graffiti
Confucius say: Man who do crossword in john have facility for words.

JOKE: "I went to a Southern doctor last week."
"How could you tell he was from the South?"
"He said 'Open your mouth and say ahhhhh will not sue.'"

September 13th

TODAY'S THOUGHT: "The art of medicine consists of amusing the patient while nature cures the disease." —*Voltaire*

OBSERVANCE/EVENT: It's "International Chocolate Day", the birthday of Milton Hershey, so all you chocoholics belly up to the bar.

Graffiti
If you can't be kind, at least be vague.

JOKE: Did you hear the one about the guy who stole the octopus from the aquarium? He was charged with eight counts of armed robbery.

September 14th

TODAY'S THOUGHT: "A vacation is what you take when you can no longer take what you've been taking." —*Earl Wilson*

OBSERVANCE/EVENT: Not to strike a sour note but "National Piano Month" is almost half over.

Graffiti
Politics makes strange bedfellows
because everybody wants the same bunk!

JOKE: A dog may be man's best friend but I don't think it works the other way around. How many of your friends have you had neutered?

September 15th

TODAY'S THOUGHT: "It took me fifteen years to discover that I had no talent for writing but I couldn't give it up, because by that time I was too famous." —*Robert Benchley*

OBSERVANCE/EVENT: Humorist Robert Benchley was born on this date in 1889.

Graffiti

Overweight people are those that live beyond their seams.

JOKE:

Q: What do you get when you cross an elephant with a nymphomaniac?

A: *A half-ton pickup*

September 16th

TODAY'S THOUGHT: "I looked up the word 'politics' in the dictionary and it's actually a combination of two words: 'poli' which means many and 'tics' which means bloodsuckers." —*Jay Leno*

OBSERVANCE/EVENT: "Smile. You're on *Candid Camera*" was said to Allen Funt as he was born on this date in 1914 in Brooklyn, New York.

Graffiti

Horror movie actors can succeed beyond their wildest screams.

JOKE: Maybe you've heard about the German student who was so naive that he thought Einstein was a single glass of beer.

September 17th

TODAY'S THOUGHT: "Marriage is nature's way of keeping people from fighting with strangers." *—Alan King*

OBSERVANCE/EVENT: Hawkeye, Radar and Klinger began what was to be an eleven year hitch on CBS as *M*A*S*H* premiered on this date in 1972.

Graffiti

Always be sure that your end justifies your jeans.

JOKE:

Q: What's the difference between a pothole and an IRS agent?

A: *You'd swerve to avoid the pothole.*

September 18th

TODAY'S THOUGHT: "Early to bed, early to rise, and your girl goes out with other guys." *—Bob Collins*

OBSERVANCE/EVENT: It's "Chiropractic Assistants Day". It's Spine Time for those fine folks who, like Kellogg's Rice Krispies, are known for their "snap, crackle and pop".

Graffiti

You can't fool all of the people all of the time.
That's why there are two political parties.

JOKE: A teenager pulled into a service station on a Vespa scooter and said, 'I'll have a pint of gas and two ounces of oil, please."
The attendant looked at him disdainfully and asked, "And would you like me to cough into your tires, sir?"

September 19th

TODAY'S THOUGHT: "Insanity is hereditary. You get it from your children." —*Joan Rivers*

OBSERVANCE/EVENT: Mary Tyler Moore first turned the world on with her smile as Mary Richards on this date in 1970. Previously she had turned the world on with her Capri slacks as Laura Petrie in *The Dick Van Dyke Show.*

Graffiti
You're only young once but you can be immature forever.

JOKE: A journeyman fighter gets knocked down. He's lying face down in the boxing ring. The ref starts to count, "One, two, three..."
The boxer's manager yells, "Don't get up until eight."
"No problem. What time is it now?"

September 20th

TODAY'S THOUGHT: "Golf, like measles, should be taught young, for, if postponed to riper years, the results may be serious." —*P.G. Wodehouse*

OBSERVANCE/EVENT: The dog days of summer aren't quite over yet. "National Dog Week" is set for the last full week in September. Naturally, they moved it about as far away as they could from "National Arbor Day".

Graffiti
Hindsight is an exact science.

JOKE: Knock, knock.
Who's there?
Arch ...
Arch who?
Gesundheit!

September 21st

TODAY'S THOUGHT: "Rock journalism is people who can't write, interviewing people who can't talk, for people who can't read." —*Frank Zappa*

OBSERVANCE/EVENT: Larry Hagman was born on this day in 1931 and it is now celebrated widely as "National Rich Villain Day", in honor of his many years of despicable deeds on *Dallas*.

Graffiti
Kleptomaniacs help themselves
because they can't help themselves.

JOKE:
Q: What do you call a Norwegian car?
A: *A Fjord*

September 22nd

TODAY'S THOUGHT: "I had the worst study habits... Then I found out what I was doing wrong. I had been highlighting with a black Magic Marker." —*Jeff Altman*

OBSERVANCE/EVENT: It's "Proposal Day", honoring unmarried adults everywhere who are seeking marriage.

Graffiti
The trouble with treating people like equals
is pretty soon they're doing the same to you.

JOKE: Guy: Will you marry me?
Girl: No.
And they lived happily ever after!

September 23rd

TODAY'S THOUGHT: "If marriage was outlawed, only outlaws would have in-laws." —*Anonymous*

OBSERVANCE/EVENT: Happy birthday to the Jetsons. The show's world premiere was on this date in 1962.

Graffiti
The Martian canals were the Martians' last ditch effort.

JOKE: Two Martians were walking through a casino when they passed a slot machine that just hit the jackpot.
As great heaps of coins were disgorged all over the floor, one Martian patted the slot on the back and said "You know, you ought to be in bed with a cold like that."

September 24th

TODAY'S THOUGHT: "Movie cowboys mystify me. How can they jump off a porch roof and onto a horse and still sing in a normal voice?" —*Bob Hope*

OBSERVANCE/EVENT: It's "Miss Piggy Day", celebrated annually on the birthday of Jim Henson, born in 1936.

Graffiti
Waste what you want not!

JOKE: Frick: My wife's really excited. She got two more credit cards this week.
Frack: Why is she so excited about a couple of credit cards?
Frick: Now she has the whole deck.

September 25th

TODAY'S THOUGHT: "Mothers mold the children's minds. Some of you have done well. There are a lot of moldy-minded kids around." —*Norm Crosby*

OBSERVANCE/EVENT: It's "National One-Hit Wonder Day", a time to salute performers like Crazy Elephant and Eddie Cooley and the Dimples.

Graffiti
Failing to prepare is preparing to fail.

JOKE: You know you're in trouble when the last thing you hear before slipping under the anesthesia is the surgeon saying "Eenie, meenie, miney, moe..."

September 26th

TODAY'S THOUGHT: "Nobody goes to that restaurant anymore. It's too crowded." —*Yogi Berra*

OBSERVANCE/EVENT: Shamu, Sea World's star attraction, was born on this date in 1985. They call the folks in charge of his party "orcanizers".

Graffiti
Sun worshippers: don't complain about sunburn... you basked for it!

JOKE: As a women's liberation zealot boarded a crowded bus, one man got to his feet.
"No, you must not give up your seat. I insist," she said.
"You can insist all you like, Lady," replied the man.
"This is my stop."

September 27th

TODAY'S THOUGHT: "One problem with growing older is that it gets progressively tougher to find a famous historical figure who didn't amount to much when he was your age." *—Bill Vaughn*

OBSERVANCE/EVENT: It's "National Good Neighbor Day" so wait until tomorrow before you start raking those leaves into your neighbor's yard.

Graffiti
A backseat driver never runs out of gas.

JOKE: Frick: My uncle just went to court on that liquor store robbery charge.
Frack: How'd he do?
Frick: He took the fifth.

September 28th

TODAY'S THOUGHT: "If you want to know how your girl will treat you after marriage, just listen to her talk to her little brother." *—Sam Levenson*

OBSERVANCE/EVENT: Al Capp, the squire of Dogpatch and creator of *Li'l Abner* was born on this day in 1909.

Graffiti
Wall Street is the capital of capital.

JOKE: Then there was the Indian chief named Running Water. He had two daughters, Hot and Cold, and a son named Luke.

September 29th

TODAY'S THOUGHT: "Hospitals are weird. They put you in a private room and then give you a public gown." —*Milton Berle*

OBSERVANCE/EVENT: This week, the week immediately preceding "Fire Prevention Week", is "Chimney Sweep Week", otherwise known as "flue season".

Graffiti

Just because love is blind
it doesn't mean that you can feel your way around.

JOKE: Did you hear about the dog that requires three baths a day? It's called a Shampoodle.

September 30th

TODAY'S THOUGHT: "Never lend your car to anyone whom you've given birth." —*Erma Bombeck*

OBSERVANCE/EVENT: Everybody's favorite modern stone-age family, *The Flintstones*, first rocked the airwaves on this date in 1960.

Graffiti

Anyone can be a winner...as long as there isn't a second entry.

JOKE: Joe: Hey, Moe, can I bum a cigarette?
Moe: I thought you quit.
Joe: I'm in phase one of quitting.
Moe: What's phase one?
Joe: I quit buying.

October 1st

TODAY'S THOUGHT: "The amount of sleep required by the average person is about five minutes more."
—Max Kauffmann

OBSERVANCE/EVENT: October 1st, 1920 gave us the Walter Matthau half of the Odd Couple while the same day in 1950 gave us the Randy half of the Quaid brothers.

Graffiti
What this country needs is more free speech worth listening to.

JOKE:

Q: What do cryogenicists sing when interring a new body?

A: *"Freeze a jolly good fellow!"*

October 2nd

TODAY'S THOUGHT: "Marriage is a wonderful institution but who wants to live in an institution?"
—Groucho Marx

OBSERVANCE/EVENT: October is "National Sarcastics Awareness Month" — yeah, like we should have told you yesterday so you'd have that whole extra day to celebrate. I mean it's soooo important...

Graffiti
Pediatricians are men of little patients.

JOKE: Did you hear the one about the guy who only told jokes in the bathroom? He was the life of the potty!

October 3rd

TODAY'S THOUGHT: "The secret of staying young is to live honestly, eat slowly and lie about your age."
—Lucille Ball

OBSERVANCE/EVENT: Sandwiched between the first and second weekends of October is "National Pickled Pepper Week". This year, as a nod to the metric system, Peter Piper will pick 8.8 liters of pickled peppers.

Graffiti
A closed mouth catches no flies.

JOKE:
Q: What kind of survey did Betsy Ross take to determine what the new U.S. banner should look like?
A: *A flag poll*

October 4th

TODAY'S THOUGHT: "Opera is when a guy gets stabbed in the back and, instead of bleeding, he sings."
—Ed Gardner

OBSERVANCE/EVENT: October is both "National Pizza Month" and "National Pasta Month" encouraging you to gorge on these high-calorie delicacies. Hope November is "National Liposuction Month".

Graffiti
They call it Middle Age because that's where it shows first.

JOKE: A guy goes to an animal auction and bids on a parrot. Every time he makes a bid, there's another bid to top him. Finally, he wins. He goes over the parrot and says, "Do you talk?"
"Who do you think's been bidding against you?"

October 5th

TODAY'S THOUGHT: "The biggest seller is cookbooks and the second is diet books — how not to eat what you just learned how to cook." —*Andy Rooney*

OBSERVANCE/EVENT: Comedian Bill Dana (who also goes by "Jose Jiminez") was born on this day in 1924.

Graffiti
Love thine enemy...it'll drive him nuts!

JOKE: In the mountains, a guy is being attacked by a mean grizzly bear. The guy's wife is standing there with a rifle, watching the bear tear his limbs off.
A hunter nearby yells, "Why don't you shoot the beast?"
"I was hoping the bear would spare me the trouble."

October 6th

TODAY'S THOUGHT: "The secret of managing is to keep the guys who hate you away from the guys who are undecided." —*Casey Stengel*

OBSERVANCE/EVENT: The first full week of October is... let's see, I had that around here somewhere...oh yeah, over here. Nope, that's not it...in the drawer maybe, no...oh, here — under the coffee mug...it's "Get Organized Week".

Graffiti
Eve gave Adam quite a ribbing.

JOKE: Wife: (to husband on couch) When are you thinking of cleaning out the garage?
Husband: In a little while, dear. Right now I'm thinking of mowing the lawn.

October 7th

TODAY'S THOUGHT: "Outside of a dog, a book is your best friend, and inside of a dog, it's too dark to read." —*Anonymous*

OBSERVANCE/EVENT: This observance may have a ring to it. On this date in 1828 the bathtub was introduced to the world.

Graffiti
Make the world beat a path to your door...take an afternoon nap!

JOKE: Frick: I gave my wife a mink for her birthday.
Frack: Did she like it?
Frick: No. She says it's a hassle to clean its cage.

October 8th

TODAY'S THOUGHT: "I majored in nursing but I had to drop it because I ran out of milk." —*Judy Tenuta*

OBSERVANCE/EVENT: It's "Take A Fall Day", in honor of Chevy Chase who stumbled his way to fame and fortune and who was born on this date in 1943.

Graffiti
You miss 100% of the shots you never take.

JOKE:

Q: What's the difference between a lawyer and a vulture?

A: *Lawyers can take off their wingtips.*

October 9th

TODAY'S THOUGHT: "I am free of all prejudices. I hate everybody equally." —*W.C. Fields*

OBSERVANCE/EVENT: October is "Auto Battery Safety Month" so if you want to get a jump on things, and really get a charge out of the occasion, you need a positive attitude especially if you're run down.

Graffiti
Procrastinators have a wait problem!

JOKE:

Q: How do you keep a simpleton in suspense?

A:

October 10th

TODAY'S THOUGHT: "There are so many TV commercials now that what used to be a simple station break sounds like a compound fracture."
—*Monta Crane*

OBSERVANCE/EVENT: Get your just desserts on "National Dessert Day", the second Thursday in October, an observance that takes the cake.

Graffiti
Save face...don't lose your head!

JOKE:

Q: What do you get when you cross a kitten with a chicken?

A: *A catapoult*

October 11th

TODAY'S THOUGHT: "The chief excitement in a woman's life is spotting women who are fatter than she is." —*Helen Rowland*

OBSERVANCE/EVENT: It's the birthday of Henry Ford and "Kiss Your Car Day". You might want to run it through the car wash first.

Graffiti
The wages of sin are usually unreported.

JOKE: Did you hear the one about the flight school that went out of business? All they offered were crash courses.

October 12th

TODAY'S THOUGHT: "She's the kind of woman who climbed the ladder of success...wrong by wrong." —*Mae West*

OBSERVANCE/EVENT: It's "International Moment Of Frustration Scream Day". Instead of moanin' and groanin' all year long, save it all up for one cathartic, psyche-cleansing moment of primal scream release.

Graffiti
Headaches are all in your mind!

JOKE: And then there was the woman with what they call an "Indiana Figure"...a large South Bend.

October 13th

TODAY'S THOUGHT: "I used to think that the human brain was the most fascinating part of the body. Then I realized, well, look what's telling me that."
—Emo Phillips

OBSERVANCE/EVENT: The second week in October is "National Pet Peeve Week", a time to vent your frustration with the thing that annoys you most... like all these silly observances.

Graffiti
People who think they know it all
really annoy those of us who do.

JOKE: Prosecutor: Why did you shoot your husband with a bow and arrow?
Defendant: I didn't want to wake the children.

October 14th

TODAY'S THOUGHT: "As a child my family's menu consisted of two choices. Take it or leave it."
—Buddy Hackett

OBSERVANCE/EVENT: It's "Be Bald And Be Free Day", a day for the hairing-impaired everywhere to buff up the old chrome dome and wear it with pride.

Graffiti
There are more important things in life than money
but none of them will go out with you if you're broke.

JOKE: Did you hear about the woman driver who went to heaven? She drove through thc Pcarly Gates and took one of them with her.

October 15th

TODAY'S THOUGHT: "No matter how bad things get you got to go on living, even if it kills you."
—*Sholom Aleichem*

OBSERVANCE/EVENT: Grumble and grouse away, it's "National Grouch Day"...a hearty "Bah, humbug!" to all.

Graffiti
Truth is stranger than fiction...at least to most people.

JOKE: A guy runs into a bar and asks the bartender, "Say, do you have a quick cure for hiccups?"
With that, the bartender gives the guy a swift kick to the stomach and says, "I bet you don't have the hiccups now, do you?"
"No," the guy grimaces, "but my buddy outside does."

October 16th

TODAY'S THOUGHT: "It's all right to hold a conversation, but you should let go of it now and then." —*Richard Armour*

OBSERVANCE/EVENT: It's "National Train Your Brain Day". Exercise those mental muscles...or just say the heck with it and kick back with a bag of Doritos and watch a Pauly Shore movie.

Graffiti
Wine is grape expectations.

JOKE: Then there was the judge who kept a mirror on the wall of his chambers. Whenever he passed it, he'd ask, "Who's the fairest of them all?"

October 17th

TODAY'S THOUGHT: "Men have a much better time of it than women; for one thing they marry later; for another thing they die earlier." —*H.L. Mencken*

OBSERVANCE/EVENT: George Wendt of *Cheers* fame got his first applause on the bottom as was the "Norm" on this day in 1948. The Lenny half of Lenny and Squiggy, Michael McKean, checked in a year earlier in 1947.

Graffiti

Keep America beautiful...throw something lovely out the window!

JOKE: Then there were the two very competitive silkworms who raced each other. It ended in a tie.

October 18th

TODAY'S THOUGHT: "I want everyone to tell me the truth, even if it costs them their job." —*Samuel Goldwyn*

OBSERVANCE/EVENT: Sitcom actress Erin Moran (Joannie on *Happy Days*) was born on this date in beautiful downtown Burbank in 1961.

Graffiti

Health food is sickening.

JOKE: Businessman: We need an accountant so we'll start you off at one hundred thousand a year.
Accountant: But you're a small company. How can you afford that?
Businessman: That's your problem now.

October 19th

TODAY'S THOUGHT: "I get my exercise running to the funerals of my friends who exercise." —*Barry Gray*

OBSERVANCE/EVENT: The Wellness Permission League says it's "Evaluate Your Life Day". Then again, as Kenny Rogers says in *The Gambler*, "never count your money while you're sittin' at the table."

Graffiti

Life is like a golf tournament...
as soon as you get out of one hole, you're heading for another.

JOKE:

Q: What's the difference between a doctor and a clergyman?

A: *One practices, the other preaches.*

October 20th

TODAY'S THOUGHT: "Fifty years ago parents were apt to have a lot of kids. Nowadays, kids are apt to have a lot of parents." —*Ernest D. Lawson*

OBSERVANCE/EVENT: It's "National Cleaner Air Week" and "National Dental Hygiene Week" so take the hint and hit the mouthwash.

Graffiti

Things are always dullest just before the yawn.

JOKE: Patient: How much will it cost for my tooth to come out?
Dentist: $100.
Patient: $100 for a minute's work? That's outrageous!
Dentist; Look, if it'll make you feel any better, I'll extract it very, very slowly.

October 21st

TODAY'S THOUGHT: "I found out why cats drink out of the toilet. My mother told me it's because it's cold in there. And I'm like: 'How did my mother know that?'" —*Wendy Liebman*

OBSERVANCE/EVENT: The third full week in October is "National Shampoo Week", the one time each year you are encouraged to work yourself into a lather.

Graffiti

How come it isn't spelled "bureaucrazy"?

JOKE: Feasting Frog #1: Where did the day go? Feasting Frog #2: Time sure is fun while you're having flies.

October 22nd

TODAY'S THOUGHT: "The reason why worry kills more people than work is that more people worry than work." —*Robert Frost*

OBSERVANCE/EVENT: Reverend Jim Ignatowski's alter-ego, Christopher Lloyd (*Taxi, Back to the Future*) was born in Stamford, Connecticut on this day in 1938.

Graffiti

Stop by for a spell. (seen in Salem, MA)

JOKE: Maybe you've heard that alimony is simply a contraction of "all his money".

October 23rd

TODAY'S THOUGHT: "A conference is a gathering of important people who singly can do nothing but together can decide that nothing can be done." —*Fred Allen*

OBSERVANCE/EVENT: "Heeeereee's Johnny!" was heard for the first time on this date in 1925 as the future "King Of Late Night", Johnny Carson was born.

Graffiti
Doctor Jekyll had something to Hyde.

JOKE: "You must be the worst caddie in the world," said the dejected golfer after a horrible day out on the links.
"I doubt it, sir," replied the caddie. "That would be too much of a coincidence."

October 24th

TODAY'S THOUGHT: "If there is a God, give me a sign!.... See, I told you that the klamaf slinfirrt gupttoorrupt..." —*Steve Martin*

OBSERVANCE/EVENT: Alonzo Phillips struck it rich as he patented matches in 1836. Here's one guy who really set the world on fire.

Graffiti
Happiness is having a clear conscience or none at all.

JOKE: A vacationer visiting Africa sees an old witch doctor lying in the road with his ear to the ground. He gets a little closer and hears the witch doctor mumbling, "Man in van, come by half an hour ago."
"Wow! You can tell that by listening to the ground?"
"No. He run over me."

October 25th

TODAY'S THOUGHT: "The average, healthy, well-adjusted adult gets up at seven-thirty in the morning feeling just plain terrible." *—Jean Kerr*

OBSERVANCE/EVENT: It's the "Sourest Day". Honor all those sourpusses out there today. You know, the ones who look as if they were weaned on a pickle.

Graffiti
Politicians are blame droppers.

JOKE:

Q: Why is consumer advocate Ralph Nader humorless?

A: *Because you can't recall a joke*

October 26th

TODAY'S THOUGHT: "The airline people are always telling you that it's safer to fly than to drive. Why don't they tell you the other statistic...that's it's safer to crash in a car than in a plane." *—Brad Stein*

OBSERVANCE/EVENT: Gary Trudeau's *Doonesbury* cartoon kicked off on this day in 1970.

Graffiti
Never ascribe to malice
that which can adequately be explained by stupidity.

JOKE:

Q: What's the only thing that can get more money out of you than the IRS?

A: *The MRS*

October 27th

TODAY'S THOUGHT: "The Soviet Union was bound to fall. It was all the way on the edge of the map."
—Married With Children's Kelly Bundy

OBSERVANCE/EVENT: On this date in 1939, *Monty Python*'s John Cleese made his first "entrance" in Weston-Super-Mare, England.

Graffiti
Support the right to arm bears.

JOKE: Diner: Waiter, why isn't there any soup on the menu?
Waiter: I wiped it off.

October 28th

TODAY'S THOUGHT: "Never brag about your ancestors coming over on the *Mayflower*. The immigration laws weren't as strict in those days." *—Lew Lehr*

OBSERVANCE/EVENT: The first baby born in flight happened high above Miami, Florida on this date in 1929. Wonder if they charged the mother for another ticket?

Graffiti
Don't lie, cheat or steal...the government hates competition.

JOKE: "How was dinner at your mother-in-law's?"
"She served me two of her specialties."
"Really? What are they?"
"Cold shoulder and hot tongue."

October 29th

TODAY'S THOUGHT: "I started out with nothing. I still have most of it." —*Michael Davis*

OBSERVANCE/EVENT: The rock-musical *Hair* opened off-Broadway in 1967. Ticket sales continued at a good clip for years.

Graffiti
Work is for people who don't know how to play golf.

JOKE: Plumber: Here's my bill for fixing that noisy heater pipe.
Homeowner: $243.11!! That's outrageous — you only tapped the pipe once! How do you figure I owe you $243.11?
Plumber: Easy...11 cents for the wear and tear on my hammer and $243 for knowing where to hit it.

October 30th

TODAY'S THOUGHT: "I haven't spoken to my wife in years. I didn't want to interrupt her."
—*Henny Youngman*

OBSERVANCE/EVENT: This was a "cool" day in 1945 as Henry Winkler (the Fonz on *Happy Days*) was born in New York City.

Graffiti
If it ain't fixed, don't broke it!

JOKE: The day Ralph retired from the Post Office, his supervisor gathered everyone together and made a little speech ending with, "Ralph, after 30 years in the United States Postal Service, what have you learned?" Ralph replied, "Don't mail my gold watch. I'll take it with me."

October 31st

TODAY'S THOUGHT: "I went to a Halloween party dressed as the equator. As people walked towards me they got warmer." —*Steven Wright*

OBSERVANCE/EVENT: The world got a very special sweet for Halloween on this date in 1950... comedic actor John Candy.

> **Graffiti**
> *Blood is thicker than water, and much tastier!*

JOKE:

Q: What do you get if you cross a pumpkin with a basketball star?

A: *A Shaq-o'-lantern*

November 1st

TODAY'S THOUGHT: "Gray hair is God's graffiti." —*Bill Cosby*

OBSERVANCE/EVENTS: It's "National Authors Day" so, in honor of the occasion, our publishers have allowed us to tell you this one — Did you hear about the guy who became a jokebook publisher only after failing as a pharmacist? He could never get the little bottles in the typewriter.

Graffiti
Vote "Yes" on Preparation H!

JOKE: Frick: My brother ran the governor's re-election campaign hoping to get a state job.
Frack: What's he doing now?
Frick: Nothing. He got the job.

November 2nd

TODAY'S THOUGHT: "A man begins cutting his wisdom teeth the first time he bites off more than he can chew." —*Herb Caen*

OBSERVANCE/EVENT: Down in Dogpatch and now in many other far-flung locales, the first Saturday in November is "Sadie Hawkins Day", a chance for the ladies to pester men for dates. Conversely, it's also a chance for men to claim that they're washing their hair or doing their nails that night.

Graffiti
Ban Graffiti!

JOKE:

Q: Who do you go to when you're Chicago, ILL?

A: *A Baltimore, M.D.*

November 3rd

TODAY'S THOUGHT: "Middle Age — when you begin to exchange your emotions for symptoms."
—S. Cobb

OBSERVANCE/EVENT: *F-Troop* veteran Ken Berry was born on this day in 1933 while another familiar sitcom face, Steve Landesberg, came along in 1945.

Graffiti
He who throws mud loses ground.

JOKE:

Q: What do politicians and criminals have in common?
A: *They take the money and run.*

November 4th

TODAY'S THOUGHT: "My grandfather always told me: 'Don't guard your money; guard your health.' While I was busy guarding my health, my grandfather stole my money." *—Jackie Mason*

OBSERVANCE/EVENT: The loveable "Naughton", Art Carney (*The Honeymooners*), was born on this date in 1918 in Mt. Vernon, New York.

Graffiti
If voting changed anything, it'd be illegal.

JOKE: Teacher: Name six animals that live in the jungle.
Student: A giraffe and five tigers

November 5th

TODAY'S THOUGHT: "The reason God made man before woman was because he didn't want any suggestions." —*Sam Levenson*

OBSERVANCE/EVENT: November is "National Football Widows Month", an observance to recognize the sacrifices of sports-spurned spouses during this, the fall and winter of their discontent.

Graffiti

When the going gets tough, the tough get prune juice.

JOKE: "How do you do well with the women?"
"The most important thing in wooing a girl is a romantic setting."
"Give me an example of a romantic setting."
"Any setting that has a diamond in it."

November 6th

TODAY'S THOUGHT: "A statesman is any politician it's considered safe to name a school after." —*Bill Vaughn*

OBSERVANCE/EVENT: *The Flying Nun*, Sally Field, was born on this date in 1946 in Pasadena, California. And that reminds us...What do you call Sister Superior when she gets to heaven? Nun of the above.

Graffiti

Two wrongs don't make a right, but three lefts will.

JOKE: Diner: Waiter, there's a footprint in my breakfast!
Waiter: Well, sir, you ordered an omelet and told me to step on it.

November 7th

TODAY'S THOUGHT: "When you are in love with someone you want to be near him all the time, except when you are out buying things and charging them to him." —*Miss Piggy*

OBSERVANCE/EVENT: The G.O.P.'s elephant was born on this day as Thomas Nast first used the pachyderm to symbolize the Republicans.

Graffiti
Woodworkers have more vices.

JOKE:

Q: Why couldn't they play cards on Noah's ark?

A: *Because the elephant sat on the deck*

November 8th

TODAY'S THOUGHT: "My grandmother started walking five miles a day when she was sixty. She's ninety-three today and we don't know where the hell she is."
—*Ellen Degeneres*

OBSERVANCE/EVENT: Believe it or not, it's "Aid and Abet Punsters Day". It's a day to laugh instead of groan at incredibly dreadful puns. The folks who founded this day claim that this is the all-time greatest triple pun: "Though he's not very humble, there's no police like Holmes."

Graffiti
Eat all you like...just don't swallow.

JOKE: Frog: Hey Waiter! There's no fly in my soup!

November 9th

TODAY'S THOUGHT: "I have no self-confidence. When girls tell me yes, I tell them to think it over." —*Rodney Dangerfield*

OBSERVANCE/EVENT: Ed Wynn, The Perfect Fool, debuted this day in 1886.

Graffiti

Never play leapfrog with a unicorn!

JOKE: Psychiatrist: Mr. Jenkins, I want you to stop smoking immediately.
Mr. Jenkins: Will that help my mental illness?
Psychiatrist: No, but you're burning a hole in my couch.

November 10th

TODAY'S THOUGHT: "This concept of marital separation is strange to me. It's like you're engaged to be divorced." —*Jerry Seinfeld*

OBSERVANCE/EVENT: MacKenzie Phillips, who played Julie on the sitcom *One Day at a Time*, took her first day at a time on this date in 1959.

Graffiti

Laugh and the world laughs with you...
snore and you sleep alone.

JOKE: Did you hear the one about the surgeon who moonlighted as a comedian? He always had everybody in stitches.

November 11th

TODAY'S THOUGHT: "Ninety percent of the game (baseball) is half mental." —*Yogi Berra*

OBSERVANCE/EVENT: Madcap Jonathan Winters improvised his first baby impression on this day in 1925.

Graffiti

Talk is cheap...
as long as it isn't lawyers who are doing the talking.

JOKE: A deer, a skunk and a duck walk into a bar. They each ask for a beer. The bartender says, "That'll be three dollars."
The deer says, "I don't have a buck."
The skunk says, "I don't have a scent."
The duck says, "Put it on my bill."

November 12th

TODAY'S THOUGHT: "Croutons are kept in a 'Stay-Fresh' pouch. How nice. Croutons are *stale bread.* If we left these open all night they could only get better. Nobody has ever gone back to the store and said, 'I need my money back. These are going fresh.'" —*Steve Bruner*

OBSERVANCE/EVENT: In 1745, a pub in Ireland hosted the world's first Happy Hour.

Graffiti

The best way to keep your word is to never give it.

JOKE: A camel walks into a bar with a mummy on its back. The mummy gets off the camel, sits on a bar stool and the bartender says, "Can I get you a drink?" The mummy says, "No, I just came here to unwind."

November 13th

TODAY'S THOUGHT: "There's a great woman behind every idiot." —*John Lennon*

OBSERVANCE/EVENT: *Soap* and *Empty Nest*'s Richard Mulligan shares this birthday with Whoopi Goldberg. He was born in 1932; she in 1949.

Graffiti
Familiarity breeds attempt.

JOKE: Two hillbillies are hunting when they come across some tracks in the woods.
"Look! Deer tracks," says the first hillbilly.
"Naah. Those are moose tracks. I know moose tracks when I see 'em," says the second hillbilly.
A few moments later they got run over by a train.

November 14th

TODAY'S THOUGHT: "Our new neighbor is so grouchy. He moved into the neighborhood the other day and was fired on by the Welcome Wagon." —*Milton Berle*

OBSERVANCE/EVENT: Two great comedic actors were born on this date: McLean Stevenson (*M*A*S*H*), in 1929 and Brian Keith (*Family Affair*), in 1921.

Graffiti
Getting caught is the mother of invention.

JOKE: A guy goes to a doctor with a duck on his head.
The doctor says, "What can I do for you?"
"I'd like this wart on my foot removed," rcplies the duck.

November 15th

TODAY'S THOUGHT: "The best way to get most husbands to do something is to suggest that perhaps they're too old to do it." —*Shirley MacLaine*

OBSERVANCE/EVENT: The folks at Pickle Packers International Inc. have come up with a real dilly — "Holidays Are Pickle Days" which runs through December 31st.

Graffiti
The average person thinks he isn't.

JOKE: "How'd you do at the track today?"
"Not so good. Not only was mine the last horse in the race, I think it was the last race in the horse!"

November 16th

TODAY'S THOUGHT: "Man is the animal that intends to shoot himself out into interplanetary space, after having given up on the problem of an efficient way to get himself five miles to work and back every day." —*Bill Vaughn*

OBSERVANCE/EVENT: We're midway through "International Drum Month" so we offer you this rimshot: "When I was five years old, my father gave me a drum and told me to beat it." —*Anonymous*

Graffiti
A female moth is a myth.

JOKE: Then there was the dog that saw a sign, WET PAINT. He did.

November 17th

TODAY'S THOUGHT: "We have nothing to fear but sanity itself." *—Mork From Ork (Mork And Mindy)*

OBSERVANCE/EVENT: *Taxi*'s Danny DeVito was born on this date in 1944.

Graffiti

If you've lost your memory, forget about it.

JOKE: On a street corner in New York a vendor waved a bouquet at a passerby. "Take home a bundle for your wife, sir."

The passerby replied, "I'm not married."

"Then take a bundle for your sweetheart."

"I don't have a girlfriend, either."

"Well, then, take home a couple of bundles to celebrate."

November 18th

TODAY'S THOUGHT: "My son has taken up meditation...at least it's better than sitting doing nothing." *—Max Kauffmann*

OBSERVANCE/EVENT: Today is the birthday of The Big Cheese himself — Mickey Mouse debuted in *Steamboat Willie* in 1928.

Graffiti

Truth is stranger than fiction but not nearly as popular.

JOKE: "I convinced my wife to marry me by promising her the sun, the moon and the stars."

"Did you keep your promise?"

"Sure did. For our honeymoon I took her to the planetarium."

November 19th

TODAY'S THOUGHT: "The best car safety device is a rear-view mirror with a cop in it." *—Dudley Moore*

OBSERVANCE/EVENT: Irked by all those little smile buttons that seem to be making a comeback lately? Well, get out and wish everyone ill on "Have A Bad Day Day". Here's hoping it's totally lousy.

Graffiti
People in cloisters shouldn't eat oysters!

JOKE: Two cannibal women are talking. One says, "I don't know what to make of my husband."
The other one says, "Get a recipe book."

November 20th

TODAY'S THOUGHT: "I bought a tube of Krazy Glue and the label fell off." *—Jay Leno*

OBSERVANCE/EVENT: Their mother's favorite Smothers Brother, Dick, was born on this date in 1938.

Graffiti
After all is said and done, there's more said than done.

JOKE: The minister droned on and on but before finally wrapping up, he apologized to the congregation for the large Band-Aid on his face. "I was so busy thinking about my sermon as I was shaving that I cut my face."
From the back came a voice, "Next time, think about shaving and cut the sermon."

November 21st

TODAY'S THOUGHT: "'Politically correct' is a contradiction in terms." —*Anonymous*

OBSERVANCE/EVENT: *That Girl*, Marlo Thomas, was born in 1938 and one of those *Laugh-In* girls, Goldie Hawn, came along in 1945.

Graffiti
The past was much like the present, only longer.

JOKE: A king was fanatical about hunting and spent virtually all of his time doing so. Finally, the people in his kingdom became fed up with his pastime and overthrew him. In all of history, this is the only known example of reign being cancelled on account of game.

November 22nd

TODAY'S THOUGHT: "I'll never forget my youth. I was teacher's pet. She couldn't afford a dog."
—*Rodney Dangerfield*

OBSERVANCE/EVENT: Rodney Dangerfield began a life of no respect on this day in 1921.

Graffiti
Shake a family tree and you're bound to get a few nuts.

JOKE: Returning from a movie intermission, a man asked the person on the aisle, "Pardon me, but did I step on your feet on the way out?"
"You certainly did," was the curt reply.
"C'mon, Honey," the man called to his wife, "this is the right row."

November 23rd

TODAY'S THOUGHT: "The phrase 'working mother' is redundant." —*Jane Sellman*

OBSERVANCE/EVENT: Harpo Marx joined the act this day in 1893.

Graffiti
Landlords aim to lease.

JOKE: A guy prays to the Lord to win the lottery, promising to do good deeds when he does. This goes on for weeks, but the guy never wins. Finally, he says, "God, I don't understand. I'm a good person. I've been praying for a long time to win the lottery. How come I haven't?"
A thundering voice from the heavens responds, "You gotta buy a ticket!"

November 24th

TODAY'S THOUGHT: "A thing worth having is a thing worth cheating for." —*W.C. Fields*

OBSERVANCE/EVENT: It's "National Bible Week". In keeping with the spirit of things, we offer this holy humor: What do you say to God when he sneezes? ...We don't know; we're just asking.

Graffiti
Always tell the truth.
Then you don't have to remember anything.

JOKE: Patient: Doc, ya gotta help me. I'm ninety years old and I still chase women.
Doctor: Sir, if you're ninety and you still chase women, you don't need my help.
Patient: I chase them but I forget why.

November 25th

TODAY'S THOUGHT: "Have you ever noticed that people who live in mobile home parks never ever move? I mean, look folks, if you're going to live in the same place for fifty years, get rid of the wheels."
—*Shashi Bhatia*

OBSERVANCE/EVENT: Comedic actor John Larroquette (*The John Larroquette Show, Night Court*) got his start this day in 1947.

Graffiti
He who hesitates is sometimes saved.

JOKE: A woman opened her refrigerator only to find Elmer Fudd inside. "What are you doing in there?" she asked.
"This is a Westinghouse, right? Well, I'm westing."

November 26th

TODAY'S THOUGHT: "Every man sees in his relatives a series of grotesque caricatures of himself."
—*H. L. Mencken*

OBSERVANCE/EVENT: Master mimic Rich Little kicked up the population of Ottawa, Canada by one today in 1938.

Graffiti
Eat, drink and be fat and drunk.

JOKE: Car Dealer: I've got bad news and worse news.
Customer: Give me the bad news first.
Car Dealer: Your car won't start.
Customer: What's the worse news?
Car Dealer: The payments won't stop.

November 27th

TODAY'S THOUGHT: "You can't judge a book by its movie." —*Anonymous*

OBSERVANCE/EVENT: The folks in Buffalo, New York didn't know it then but the man who would make it "Howdy Doody Time", Buffalo Bob Smith, was born there on this date in 1917.

Graffiti

Golddiggers are gimmie pigs!

JOKE: A psychiatrist says to his new patient, "Why don't you start at the beginning?"
"Alright. In the beginning I created the heavens and the earth..."

November 28th

TODAY'S THOUGHT: "I hate the outdoors. To me the outdoors is where the car is." —*Will Durst*

OBSERVANCE/EVENT: The first skywriting exhibition was given over New York City in 1922. It read, "Should have brought seat belt or parachute..."

Graffiti

The best way to live happily ever after
is on a day-to-day basis.

JOKE: Fred spotted his old chum Bill at a high school reunion and asked him how things have been going.
"I married my high school sweetheart. It was puppy love," said Bill.
"How's it working out?"
"It's been a dog's life ever since."

November 29th

TODAY'S THOUGHT: "I like long walks, especially when they are taken by people who annoy me." —*Fred Allen*

OBSERVANCE/EVENT: Larry Sander's alter-ego, Garry Shandling, did his first monologue ("Waaaaaah!") on this date in 1949 and Howie Mandel debuted in '55.

Graffiti
Do rivers sleep in river beds?

JOKE: "My wife says if I don't give up golf, she'll leave me."
"Gee, that's a tough break."
"Yeah, I'm sure going to miss her."

November 30th

TODAY'S THOUGHT: "There's something neat about a sweater with a hole. It makes you look like a tough guy." —*Beaver Cleaver*

OBSERVANCE/EVENT: It's "Stay Home Because You're Well Day". What fun is it staying home when you're sick? Call in well and enjoy your robust good health. (Please note that *The Bathroom Joke Almanac* is not responsible for any adverse effect on your career should you choose to observe this holiday.)

Graffiti
Ancestry is hereditary.

JOKE: Did you hear the one about the guy who froze to death? He went to a movie drive-in to see "Closed For Winter".

December 1st

TODAY'S THOUGHT: "I think crime pays. The hours are good. You travel a lot." —*Woody Allen*

OBSERVANCE/EVENT: Woody Allen began accumulating neuroses this day in 1935 and Richard Pryor came along in 1940.

Graffiti

Show me a man who's afraid of Christmas and I'll show you a Noel Coward.

JOKE:

Q: Why are the colors of Christmas green and red?

A: *Because you spend all your green and wind up in the red*

December 2nd

TODAY'S THOUGHT: "When I was a kid, one cop could have taken care of the whole neighborhood. Now, one cop wouldn't be safe in the neighborhood."
—*Mike Royko*

OBSERVANCE/EVENT: On this date in 1933, Bertil Clason and Sigrid Carlson were wed in the first transatlantic telephone wedding. (Talk about "phoning it in"!)

Graffiti

Mickey Mouse has Disney spells.

JOKE: Wife: I'm going out to do some Christmas shopping. I have to pick up some snoo.
Husband: What's snoo?
Wife: Not much. What's snoo with you?

December 3rd

TODAY'S THOUGHT: "There is never enough time — unless you're serving it." —*Malcolm Forbes*

OBSERVANCE/EVENT: It's "Bake A Biscuit Day", celebrated on the birthday of Charles Pillsbury. Since the holidays are almost upon us, feel free to substitute cookies.

Graffiti
The purpose of life is a life of purpose.

JOKE: Shirley came home to find a card taped to her door which read "Merry Christmas from the custodial staff."
"How nice," she thought. A week later she again found a card taped to her door. It read, "Merry Christmas from the custodial staff — *Second Notice.*"

December 4th

TODAY'S THOUGHT: "My grandfather's been senile all his life but nobody ever told me and I've been taking all his advice." —*Steve Sweeny*

OBSERVANCE/EVENT: Max Baer Jr., Jethro of *The Beverly Hillbillies*, was born in Oakland, California on this date in 1937.

Graffiti
Astrology is Taurus.

JOKE: Diner: Waiter! You're thumb is in my soup!
Waiter: Don't worry, sir. It isn't hot.

December 5th

TODAY'S THOUGHT: "Scientists announced today that they have found a cure for apathy. However, they claim no one has shown the slightest bit of interest in it."
—George Carlin

OBSERVANCE/EVENT: Today marks "Bathtub Party Day", a time to immerse yourself in a long, hot bath. (Better yet, save water; bathe with a friend.)

Graffiti
Boys will be boys...and so will a lot of middle-aged men.

JOKE: Frick: I'm in big trouble with my girlfriend. She showed the engagement ring I gave her to the girls at work.
Frack: Didn't they admire it?
Frick: Admire it? Half of them recognized it.

December 6th

TODAY'S THOUGHT: "I was walking down the street wearing glasses when the prescription ran out."
—Steven Wright

OBSERVANCE/EVENT: Steven Wright began putting together his bent view of reality on this day in 1955.

Graffiti
How can they say God is dead...
we're not even sure about Elvis.

JOKE: A guy goes up to a Salvation Army Santa and asks, "Do you save sinners?"
"Why yes, we do."
"Great," says the guy throwing ten bucks in the kettle. "Save me a couple for Saturday night!"

December 7th

TODAY'S THOUGHT: "Claustrophobia: fear of Santa Claus." —*Anonymous*

OBSERVANCE/EVENT: Sports fans rejoice; the instant replay was first introduced on this date in 1963. Sports fans rejoice; the instant replay was first introduced on this date in 1963.

Graffiti
Santa's helpers are subordinate clauses.

JOKE: Boss: What's this $397 on your expense voucher?
Salesman: That's my restaurant bill.
Boss: Well, don't buy any more restaurants.

December 8th

TODAY'S THOUGHT: "A lawyer is a gentleman who rescues your estate from your enemies and keeps it for himself." —*Lord Brougham*

OBSERVANCE/EVENT: Flip Wilson perfected his first delivery on this day in 1933.

Graffiti
With age comes wisdom...
like the wisdom to start lying about your age.

JOKE: Frack: My mother sent me two sweaters for Christmas and she stopped by while I was wearing one.
Frick: So what's the problem?
Frack: As soon as she saw me, she started in with, "What's the matter? You don't like the other one?"

December 9th

TODAY'S THOUGHT: "By all means marry. If you get a good wife you will become happy...and if you get a bad one you will become a philosopher." *—Socrates*

OBSERVANCE/EVENT: St. Louis, Missouri welcomed Redd Foxx into the world on this date in 1922.

Graffiti
TV repeats are rerun of the mill.

JOKE: Miss Crabtree: Children, because of the holiday season, we will only have half a day of school this morning.
Pupils: Hooray!
Miss Crabtree: Then we'll have the other half this afternoon.

December 10th

TODAY'S THOUGHT: "Whenever I date a guy, I think 'Is this the man I want my children to spend their weekends with?'" *—Rita Rudner*

OBSERVANCE/EVENT: It's "15 Days Until Christmas Day" and, as you're doing your holiday shopping, remember: It's better to give than to receive. That way you don't have to bother exchanging it.

Graffiti
Beauty is only sin deep!

JOKE: When we opened a new Christmas club we got a toaster from the bank. Every day at three o'clock it stops working.

December 11th

TODAY'S THOUGHT: "Every crowd has a silver lining." —*P.T. Barnum*

OBSERVANCE/EVENT: December is "Bingo's Birthday Month", a time to celebrate the invention of Bingo in 1929 by Edwin S. Lowe. Accordingly, we bring you this..."Bingo" is the answer. And the question...What one word can you say to make a roomful of little old ladies cuss?

Graffiti

Help! I'm having an out of money experience.

JOKE: There are three periods in a man's life: he believes in Santa Claus; he doesn't believe in Santa Claus; he is Santa Claus.

December 12th

TODAY'S THOUGHT: "Democracy means that anyone can grow up to be president and anyone who doesn't grow up can be vice-president." —*Johnny Carson*

OBSERVANCE/EVENT: Hoboken's favorite son and Doonesbury's favorite target, Frank Sinatra, was born on this date in 1915. The Chairman of the Board's birthday inspires the graffiti you see below.

Graffiti

To do is to be — Rousseau.
To be is to do — Sartre.
Doobedoobedoo — Sinatra.

JOKE: Did you hear the one about the Zen Master's office? He had an inner calm installed.

December 13th

TODAY'S THOUGHT: "There's not much good in the worst of us, and so many of the worst of us get the best of us, that the rest of us aren't even worth talking about."—*Gracie Allen*

OBSERVANCE/EVENT: Multi-talented comedic performer Dick Van Dyke entered the world smiling on this date in 1925.

Graffiti

What's the digital version of "counterclockwise"?

JOKE: Did you the hear the one about the family who put up an artificial Christmas tree? When they got up Christmas morning, all the presents under the tree were fake.

December 14th

TODAY'S THOUGHT: "By the time my father was my age he had served in the war, built a house, raised a family. My greatest accomplishment so far is having all five *Planet Of The Apes* films on tape." —*Larry Miller*

OBSERVANCE/EVENT: Patty Duke, who would go on to play identical cousins Patty and Cathy Lane on *The Patty Duke Show*, made her world debut on this date in 1946.

Graffiti

Rain dance Friday night...weather permitting.

JOKE:

Q: Why does Santa use reindeer to pull his sleigh?

A: *Because the elephants kept crashing through the roof*

December 15th

TODAY'S THOUGHT: "It doesn't matter whether you win or lose until you lose." —*Anonymous*

OBSERVANCE/EVENT: That Dorf guy, Tim Conway, was born in 1933.

Graffiti
You can't shake hands with a closed fist.

JOKE: A parrot, a parakeet and a mynah bird go into a bar. They order three beers. The bartender comes back with two beers, one for the parrot and one for the parakeet.
The mynah bird complains, "Hey, where's my beer?"
The bartender says, "Sorry, we don't serve mynahs here."

December 16th

TODAY'S THOUGHT: "This guy is so cheap he sends out one Christmas card each year... in the form of a chain letter." —*Phyllis Diller*

OBSERVANCE/EVENT: It's "Eat What You Want Day". Hey, it's the holidays, knock yourself out.

Graffiti
Crash the house party...barge in.

JOKE: Two hillbillies were having a conversation. The first hillbilly says, "You know, it's a dog-eat-dog world out there."
The second one says, "Yeah, but it could be worse. It could be the other way around."

December 17th

TODAY'S THOUGHT: "I hate the word "star". Do you know what "star" spells backwards?" *—Hugh O'Brian*

OBSERVANCE/EVENT: Today is "Wright Brothers Day" in honor of the inventors of the airplane. We can thank them for the gift of flight, airline food, lost luggage and interminable delays.

Graffiti
Let things go to pot. Take a coffee break.

JOKE: 'Tis the season and some airlines have begun putting mistletoe at the baggage counters. That way you can kiss your luggage good-bye.

December 18th

TODAY'S THOUGHT: "Parents were invented to keep children happy by giving them something to ignore." *—Ogden Nash*

OBSERVANCE/EVENT: Movie producer/director Steven Spielberg was born on this date in 1947. In honor of the occasion, we present this groaner: How many letters are there in the alphabet? 24...ET went home.

Graffiti
Sunbathing is a fry in the ointment.

JOKE: Husband: Doc, ya gotta help me out. My wife thinks she's a rubber band.
Psychiatrist: Don't worry, she'll soon snap out of it.

December 19th

TODAY'S THOUGHT: "I'll tell you what I don't like about Christmas office parties: looking for a new job afterward." —*Phyllis Diller*

OBSERVANCE/EVENT: It's "Can't Get Up Day". Remember those "Help! I've fallen and I can't get up" commercials? This observance marks their 1985 debut. Lay on the floor and yell for your relatives to bring you things today.

Graffiti

Boat shows have a yacht to offer.

JOKE: There's a new item out there for gift-giving. It's a battery-operated battery. The only problem is the batteries aren't included.

December 20th

TODAY'S THOUGHT: "If you drink like a fish, don't drive. Swim." —*Joe E. Lewis*

OBSERVANCE/EVENT: It's "I've Got My Big Fat Guy Pants On Day". (Enjoy it while you can. After the holidays it may no longer be optional.)

Graffiti

Anyone who isn't thoroughly confused obviously doesn't understand the situation.

JOKE: Doctor: I have some good news and some bad news.
Patient: What's the bad news?
Doctor: We're going to have to operate on you.
Patient: Jeez, what could be the good news?
Doctor: I bowled a 300 yesterday.

December 21st

TODAY'S THOUGHT: "The whole world isn't watching anymore. It's renting videos instead." *—Julia Willis*

OBSERVANCE/EVENT: This date in 1914 brought the first feature length film comedy, *Tillie's Punctured Romance.*

Graffiti
Custer was Siouxed.

JOKE: Father: I got Johnny a little plastic machine gun with a grenade launcher and bayonet. It comes with the Little Commando Tactical Nuclear Anti-Personnel Missile.
Mother: That's a terrible gift for Christmas!
Father: What's the matter? I wrapped it in paper that says "Peace On Earth".

December 22nd

TODAY'S THOUGHT: "What you don't know would make a great book." *—Sydney Smith*

OBSERVANCE/EVENT: The Beaver's mom, June Cleaver, (aka Barbara Billingsley) was born on this date in 1922.

Graffiti
Recapture your youth. Cut off his allowance!

JOKE: "So, Al, I never asked you. How come you had fourteen kids?"
"Well, Pete, my wife always took her hearing aid off before bedtime and as we turned in I always asked her 'So...you want to go to sleep or what?' And she'd always say, 'What?'"

December 23rd

TODAY'S THOUGHT: "If I were two-faced would I be wearing this one?" —*Abe Lincoln*

OBSERVANCE/EVENT: Before the month's out, *The Bathroom Almanac* would like to remind you that this is "Safe Toys and Gifts Month" and to take this opportunity for the following: What was the first thing the rich kid built when he got an erector set for Christmas? A tax shelter.

Graffiti

Running is unnatural...
except from predators and to the bathroom.

JOKE: "I've finally discovered the magic of Christmas."
"What is it?"
"It's what makes your money disappear."

December 24th

TODAY'S THOUGHT: "In suggesting gifts: money is appropriate, and one size fits all."
—*William Randolph Hearst*

OBSERVANCE/EVENT: It's Christmas Eve. (And those three words just happen to be the answer to "What did Adam say to Eve on December 25th?")

Graffiti

The trouble with the straight and narrow
is that there's no place to park.

JOKE: Frick: For Christmas, I bought my son a toy that was guaranteed to be completely unbreakable.
Frack: What happened?
Frick: He used it to break all his other toys.

December 25th

TODAY'S THOUGHT: "Santa Claus has the right idea: visit people once a year." —*Victor Borge*

OBSERVANCE/EVENT: It's Christmas Day and you can't hide in the bathroom all day. No matter how long you stay, your relatives will still be there when you come out!

Graffiti

Beatnik: Santa Claus on Christmas Day.

JOKE: Knock, knock.
Who's there?
Dexter...
Dexter who?
Dexter halls with boughs of holly...

December 26th

TODAY'S THOUGHT: "The trouble with children is that they are not returnable." —*Quentin Crisp*

OBSERVANCE/EVENT: It's "National Whiners Day", for those poor souls who whine on line while returning gifts.

Graffiti

Be sincere even if you have to fake it.

JOKE: Coach: OK, Quincy — you can be the end, guard and tackle.
Quincy: Great, Coach! How do I do that?
Coach: Sit at the end of the bench — guard the water bucket and tackle anyone who gets near it.

December 27th

TODAY'S THOUGHT: "You know you're getting old when you stoop to tie your shoes and wonder what else you can do while you're down there." —*George Burns*

OBSERVANCE/EVENT: Hey, boys and girls...It was *Howdy Doody* time for the first time on this date in 1947.

Graffiti

Be an organ donor. Give a heart to a lawyer!

JOKE: A man goes to a psychiatrist and tells him that he bites his nails all the time.

The shrink says, "That's not the worst thing in the world."

"But I'm a carpenter."

December 28th

TODAY'S THOUGHT: "I've been on a calendar, but I've never been on time." —*Marilyn Monroe*

OBSERVANCE/EVENT: The end of the calendar year is almost upon us, so lest we forget, this is "International Calendar Awareness Month". Hence, "Today's Thought".

Graffiti

Thank God I am an atheist!

JOKE:

Q: What did the Siamese twins ask for at the golf course?

A: *Tee for two*

December 29th

TODAY'S THOUGHT: "Work is the greatest thing in the world so we should always save some of it for tomorrow." *—Don Herold*

OBSERVANCE/EVENT: Two of TV's great series stars share today as a birthday: Mary Tyler Moore was born in 1937 and Ted Danson drew cheers from his family in 1947.

Graffiti
Conserve electricity. Thanks a watt!

JOKE: Newlywed: My wife worships me.
Pal: How do you know that?
Newlywed: She places burnt offerings before me three times a day.

December 30th

TODAY'S THOUGHT: "The wedding march always reminds me of the music played when soldiers go into battle." *—Heinrich Heine*

OBSERVANCE/EVENT: The multi-talented funny lady Tracey Ullman was born on this date in 1959 in Buckinghamshire, England.

Graffiti
Dieters: a word to the wides is sufficient.

JOKE: Applicant: My father lent me $100,000 for my law education and after my first case, I paid him back every dime.
Personnel Director: That's quite impressive. What case was that?
Applicant: He sued me for it.

December 31st

TODAY'S THOUGHT: "New Year's Eve — that's when your guests pass out at about the same time as the old year!" —*Anonymous*

OBSERVANCE/EVENT: It's "No Resolution Day". Make up your mind to make no New Year's resolutions. Of course if you do that, you've already made a New Year's resolution. Go figure.

Graffiti

Betty Crocker is a flour-child!

JOKE: Then there was the guy whose New Year's resolution was to start giving up giving up.